Beneath The Winds of War

Pola Wawer

Producer & International Distributor
eBookPro Publishing
www.ebook-pro.com

Beneath the Winds of War
Original book title (Polish): Poza Gettem I Obozem

The book has been published with support from Ministry of Culture and Art

Translation from the Polish by Kasia Stewart

Contact info:
itzhakpreiss@gmail.com
agency@ebook-pro.com

ISBN 9789655752861

For dear Guta and Jeshua, I am finally sending you these memories of the worst years of my life, when I was still together with Sierioża and Rózia.

Pola
Warsaw January 1944

For those who helped me not only survive but also to keep my faith in man.

In memory of my parents
Maria and Don Komaj

BENEATH THE WINDS OF WAR

POLA WAWER

Contents

Foreword

After nearly half a century, memories from the worst years of my life are coming back – to the occupation – to bear witness to some facts and to save from oblivion mainly people and their actions, thanks to which my mom and I, out of the five members of our immediate family, were rescued from the horrors of war.

What was different about our occupation story was that we, without having any resources or "Aryan papers," were saved, thanks to the help of many people of good will. These people were of various nationalities, beliefs, education and social status. A sense of human solidarity was their only common trait. Some of these people have passed away, some disappeared from my horizon during the confusing border changes on the road to repatriation. With others I managed to keep in close or distant, frequent or scarce, contact, for years. All of them stayed in my grateful memory for the rest of my life, although in too many cases I was not able to express this at the right time.

I worked a lot and was very busy. In the course of ongoing daily tasks and experiences, things got lost. Things, though in the past, which are yet still important and always relevant. This is not a justification, but perhaps it explains it a little bit. There were also some external circumstances that would have made writing down these memories difficult. I'm doing it now in the hope that nevertheless, it is not too late.

Remnants of an Old Life

My former life had been irrevocably lost by the end of summer, 1939. The war had been hanging in the air for some time. It was at the forefront of everyone's minds and people were afraid. The older ones who had survived the First World War saw this new one in a different form. They remembered the past horrors they had endured and concentrated on how to prepare for this new struggle. The younger ones usually lacked the awareness to comprehend both what had happened and what was coming. Patriotic propaganda attempted to inspire uncompromising loyalty in people to their country, to build faith in the strength of our military forces. The war was the main topic of the day, and featuring in projections, horoscopes, and more.

Still, our daily life during this beautiful summer went on as usual.

We lived at the summer resort in Wołokumpia, near Vilnius, in a house on a large forest plot that had been remodeled by my father in the preceding year. My parents, having braved many hard and lean years, were now quite wealthy. Mom, who had a Russian high school examination certificate and a French Doctor of Medicine diploma, had to also complete a series of abridged Polish high school examinations (language, literature, history, geography, knowledge of Poland) in order to validate her qualifications.

Being a doctor with eight years' experience of professional independent work in Ukraine, she put in years of hard work to acquire the privilege to practice medicine, which coincided with my graduation from the gymnasium. In the early thirties, all this was behind her and she had an flourishing private gynecology practice.

Father, who came from the area surrounding Kharkov in Ukraine, already knew the Polish language, was accustomed to the Polish culture and ran his own electrotechnical office. He was an electrotechnical and mechanical engineer. He built power stations, electric and steam windmills, and he also established an energy network in the Vilnius region.

They both had good wages.

We lived in the house inherited by my mom and her two sisters from my grandmother. It had only three apartments, one for each sister. Ours was the largest because Father was always redeveloping and adding something to it. When we moved there in 1924, it had only two rooms with a kitchen but by the time the war broke out, it was a seven-room apartment that housed both Mom's surgery clinic and Father's office.

I'd just graduated from my studies and completed a compulsory training period. I had begun a residency in the ophthalmology department at the railway hospital. My husband, Sierioża Wincygster, had completed his medical studies two years before I had and was specializing in neurology. Neither of us was earning any money yet.

My husband's sister, Rózia, also lived with us. In the early thirties, she was a part of "Szomr," a left-wing Zionist youth organization. After completing her training, she immigrated to Palestine, which at that time was a British territory. After some time, she joined a communist party, and was later arrested and deported to Poland. She moved in with her family in Łódź. As a communist, she struggled to find employment in Łódź. My family invited her into our home. Thanks to their support, she completed nurse and midwifery school and in 1939 was working as a mental health nurse in Deksznie. A professor of psychiatry from Stefan Batory University in Vilnius founded such mental health centers in Deksznie and Łejpuny, where patients who were deemed to not be a danger to the community lived freely with local peasant families and did such minor household or farm jobs that their abilities allowed; they were looked after by a nurse living in the village in a subsidised apartment who would also run a first aid pharmacy and carry out tasks for non-resident psychiatrists from the clinic.

Another member of the family was Nadia, who had lived with us for twelve years until she got married. Father called her the Minister of Internal Affairs because she liked to know about everything, to interfere with and to influence every household affair, and fiercely protected our family business.

The house was full of work, busyness, youth, friendships, laughter, singing and other things alike. This atmosphere was my parents' gift to me – a source from which I drew joy to the full in the good times and strength to survive when the worst came.

My parents' marriage survived many difficult life trials – scarcity when both were students, two years of separation during the First World War, difficult times during the revolution in Ukraine and more.

They came to Vilnius when they were already in their thirties, and it took them a long time to establish the fundamentals of an independent life. This didn't help them in forming connections with local, long-time residents. They managed to make some acquaintances and friendships, but their true community was our friends. I suspect that besides the circumstances that debilitated them there was quite a bit of their own consideration involved. Looking back, it seems to me that in their own way, they had a desire to create cross-generational relationships. Thanks to them, a unique, rare at that time, and probably uncommon even now, community came into existence. A community without generational distance. We preferred to spend our free time together and no subjects were taboo.

I was the only child; however, the house was always full of young people. They would happily spend time equally with my parents and me and sometimes even with them without me.

The youngest at heart in our large circle was infallibly Father, always ready for tricks, jokes, adventures, singing and playing.

"Come on oldies, let's sing. I see that you are getting bored," and soon he began to chant one of the many songs he knew.

"Just remember, not in unison," he reminded them. He was a high tenor and had a good ear for music.

He happily played chess with us and in summer, croquet.

While playing croquet sometimes we had such bad arguments about suspected rule-breaking or point calculation that Mom had to intervene.

"Don't embarrass yourself, after all, you are almost old," she would say, or tell me off: "You are behaving like a child. After all, you are a doctor and a married woman!"

Mom was sensible, cautious, reflective, level-headed. The backbone of the family. It was hard to unbalance her or make her angry. However, if it happened, she could be angry or sulk for such a long time that Father couldn't even remember what for.

It was incredibly funny and if their conversations were held in public, it made people laugh.

"How is it that you have so much goodness in you?" Mom would finally surrender.

"I get it from my mother," Father would become serious. Such scenes could unfold in various forms and at their end, the air would clear just like after a thunderstorm, though thunderstorms were rare.

Whilst Father's domain was games, singing, adventures and the likes, Mom's specialty was storytelling – about her family home, school years and difficult times as a student, although these in some ways were still fun and colorful. She also told us about her life as a junior doctor, stories that were especially enjoyed by my fellow university friends.

I wasn't aware then what beautiful pearls of wisdom Mom was bestowing on us. All that surrounded me seemed so ordinary, normal; Mom is like she is, and Father is like he is.

This 1939 summer seemed like any other ordinary summer, the same as the previous ones, albeit particularly sunny.

We were still living in the summer resort and on the 1st of September we made plans to go into town – my parents to work, we to our commitments. We were sitting in the car waiting for Father, who'd gone back to the house to get something. At that moment, two officers appeared at the gate and asked for Father. When he turned up on the veranda, this short conversation took place between them:

"Engineer Don Komaj?"

"Yes."

"Can we see your identity card, please? Is that your car?"

"Yes, it's mine"

"This is a warrant. By twelve o'clock today, it must be submitted to the army and delivered to this address."

"Is this a precaution in case of a war?" asked Father.

"It is no longer merely a precaution."

That was how we found out that war had broken out.

We struggled to make our way to the house in Vilnius because the road leading to the city was full of soldiers and the newly conscripted who were traveling to Vilnius on farm wagons.

Days of horror followed as from the west and the east, two hostile armies, Soviets and Germans, advanced towards each other, with us in the middle. We were uncertain whether we would soon find ourselves on the front line.

Vilnius was taken by the Soviet army.

This period, which for many was a time of difficult experiences, didn't have much of an impact on our lives. After the community health service was set up, Mom took a job at the mother and child clinic and Father was employed to renovate and rebuild the Kurlandzka oil mill in Vilnius. We youngsters remained at our jobs. But we already knew what was happening in Łódź after the Germans had taken it, and about the fate of people from that region, particularly Jews.

Even before the war in 1939, my husband Sierioża followed political and military developments with great anxiety and predicted the worst.

I remember one of our conversations at the table. A world exhibition was being held in the United States and we were talking about it.

"What do you think about selling everything or almost everything we have here and going to the exhibition in the United States, taking into account that if the war breaks out, we will be able to stay there and will have some resources to start over? After all, we have our professions. And if war does not break out, we will decide what to do then," asked Sierioża.

My parents looked at Sierioża like he'd lost his mind.

"Are you joking or serious?"

"Totally serious," he replied.

"So you are suggesting that we give up all that we have achieved through such hard work and start everything over from scratch?"

The more information we received from occupied territories, especially concerning his family in Łódź, the more Sierioża became concerned. He was petrified by the thought of what was coming to Vilnius and its people, to Jews, to us. He made contact with runaways, held many conversations and was constantly trying to get a sense of what was going on over there and predict what would be coming here.

Lately, as I was writing this memoir, I found out from his niece that with permission from my parents, he had sent someone to Łódź to get his family out through the border to us, to Vilnius. It was unbelievable but Sierioża's sister decided not to go because it was quite cold, and she was worried that the children would get sick. It's hard to judge today whether it was a good or bad decision. Of the whole family, only the niece whom I mentioned earlier and who survived the Łódź ghetto, Auschwitz, two other camps on the way and Ravensbruck, survived.

Who knows what would have happened if they had managed to reach us? There is no answer to this question.

Meanwhile, Mom, who had learned from her experience of the First World War, was stockpiling food to prepare for the war – buying flour, sugar, dry sausage, making fruit preserves and anything else she could manage. Her husband watched her thoughtful hustle with compassion and suppressed irony.

"I'm not sure, Mareczka, if we will ever use your supplies. But surely someone will benefit from them."

Mom was convinced that this "child" understood nothing, because what could he possibly remember from the war? She would tease him:

"We'll see how happy you will be to eat it."

At that time, Sierioża and I went to Estonia. It was a business trip for Sierioża – he was escorting a patient to a consultation in Tallinn and I used this opportunity to see Tallinn and Riga.

In Tallinn we met local Jews. There was a lot of anxiety and uncertainty about the future amongst them. Many were leaving Estonia and crossing over on fishing boats to Finland and Sweden, where they hoped to be safer. They advised us strongly against returning to Vilnius and offered us help with crossing over to Sweden.

This shook us, but we had no doubts about the course of action we should take – we knew we had to get back home and make momentous decisions such as these together with our parents and Rózia.

The journey back was very difficult. Trains to Riga were overflowing – military transports were heading west. Passenger trains ran infrequently and practically unscheduled. Countless crowds of people streamed through the city in all possible directions. The war migration had begun.

We arrived in Vilnius physically and mentally exhausted; the mood and atmosphere there was very depressing. All people talked about was the military conflict between Germany and the Soviet Union. There was an endless struggle to get hold of any radio news reports, which were often contradictory and confusing.

Not long after our return, a gentleman from Riga arrived with a message from my cousin in England, Lowa Benari. The writing was short, sort of like a telegraph: "Leave everything, trust my messenger and come with him – we will be together."

We didn't take this opportunity, either. I can't remember what our decision was based on. I suspect *ex post*[1] that we lacked imagination, perhaps courage too, to leave our semi-functioning home and to go out into the unknown. Soon after, my cousin sent another messenger to me: "I'm not surprised that you understand nothing, but Uncle? Re-think your decision. I'm waiting." We didn't rethink, we stayed.

The next contact with my cousin took place in 1946, when he found us, only he knows how, in Bielsko, Silesia.

---

1   "after the fact" (Latin)

Leaving Our Home and Vilnius

The German-Soviet war broke out on the 22nd of June 1941. Vilnius was con-
quered by the fascist army. The tanks were spread out right in front of our
flat, in a large, undeveloped, triangular area. The soldiers were resting after
a tiring march. In the morning they shaved, cleaned themselves carefully
and talked joyfully. Their conversations were noisy, and apparently full of
amusement for them because they were often punctuated by uncontrollable
laughter. From dawn to dusk you could hear their free, loud, coarse voices.
Even though people didn't yet know what to expect, sidewalks in the area
were empty – nearby streets were avoided just in case. Even the most curious
of kids didn't approach them, at most they observed from their windows
or balconies. One of the sides of this triangular aera was occupied by tiny
Jewish shops, where items like flour, hulled grains, vegetables, poultry, and
feathers were traded. Since the tanks were located there, barely any of them
were open for more than a few hours a day. Their owners were visibly scared
of their new neighbors, remembering their experiences from the pogroms
during the brief Smetona regime when people had broken into their shops,
ripped open sacks of goods and scattered their contents around the street.

People lived anxiously, expecting a disaster.

On one of the first days of the occupation we were walking home on
Zahalka street. The weather was nice and sunny. Our arms were linked, and
we were talking and laughing. A German officer was walking towards us.
As he overtook us, he suddenly swung a whip in the air and with great force

struck Father across his face. Our happy conversation was cut by that whip, we paused mid-sentence, our voices stuck in our throats, and we stopped. We heard a pedestrian whisper behind us: "Keep walking like nothing has happened." We followed his advice with a great effort. I huddled with Father in silence, and we walked on.

I was raised without violence, nobody at home had ever raised a hand to me, not even to threaten. But this man had struck Father, leaving an angry red lash mark on his face! It was something beyond belief, something impossible to grasp. Silently, avoiding each other's eyes like we were embarrassed about what had taken place, we returned home. I locked myself in my room and wept. When I came out with eyes swollen from crying, Father was lying down with a cold compress on his face, Mom was hugging and kissing him, not even wiping her own tears as they rolled down her face. Rózia was sitting next to them, totally petrified as she stroked his legs.

We were slowly beginning to comprehend what *Ubermensch* meant – the superior race.

What had made him so furious? Perhaps it was simply the sight of ordinarily-dressed, upright and, how dare they, laughing slaves that enraged him.

This incident changed the atmosphere at home for good – the sense of uncertainty deepened, a taste of something horrifying, unknown, unimaginable.

Sierioża's family, his older sister with her husband and two children, were in the Łódź ghetto. For a long time we kept in touch through letters, at first even via the official postal service. Later on, we found out about them from short messages sent by escapees, who poured into the area in large numbers from Warsaw, Białystok and Łódź. With them came more accurate news about the territories occupied by the Nazis.

However, still the Bekantmachtung[2] for Jews banning them from using the sideways, the compulsory armbands and early curfews, came as a huge shock.

One day, all of us but Father were fired from our jobs.

At that time, Father was overseeing some rebuilding or remodelling work

---

2   "announcement" (German)

at the Kurlandzka oil mill, a job that had been contracted by Soviet authorities. The Germans gave orders for the work to continue. Mr. Władysław Frąckiewicz worked together with Father at the oil mill as well as on other contracts as a technician.

We just couldn't imagine Father decorated with an armband, marching through the city's cobblestones to its outskirts where the oil mill was located. Father had grown up in the Ukrainian grasslands, spent time as a student in France as a political emigrant from tsarist Russia amongst its progressive youth; now he was expected to step back to the Middle Ages. How could he survive this?

The night before Father's first march with the new social status of a slave, we barely slept. But still everyone tried to appear composed not to worsen what must have been a nightmarish situation for him already.

Father started work quite early, at about 7am. He was almost ready to leave when someone rang the bell. It was Mr. Władysław Frąckiewicz.

"What's wrong, Mr. Frąckiewicz?"

"Nothing, engineer Komaj, let's go together, it will be more cheerful," we heard the reply to Father's question.

"But Mr. Frąckiewicz, this makes no sense. It is not going to help me, and it can only hurt you. It's hard to predict what they will do."

"I don't care. If you can walk on these cobblestones, so can I."

He didn't back down. For a few days, he marched next to Father, small, slim, proud. It took a long time and lots of effort to persuade him to stop these daily demonstrations of human solidarity and contempt towards our occupiers.

In these first days of hell, Priest Jankowski from the nearby parish of All Saints Church located at the corner of Zawalna and Rudnicka streets, unexpectedly paid us a visit. I don't know if he knew Father before that; probably not. He offered "neighborly" assistance with sorting out matters in the city, should we need it. At that time we didn't need anything, but both Mr. Frąckiewicz as well as Priest Jankowski kept this attitude throughout the whole occupation and later on, we used their help. These first spontaneous expressions of respect for human dignity, and of solidarity with those who were deprived of their basic rights, were just as meaningful as was their later help. They sowed faith in people, in us, and seeds of hope for survival, which gave us strength to keep going.

What were we to do once they set up a ghetto? At that time, the early curfew gave us opportunity for long discussions on the subject.

"We can't let them lock us in the ghetto. We need to keep a bit of independence, a chance to make our own decisions. We might need to leave the house, maybe even Vilnius," Sierioża had a clear view of what we must do.

He was so deeply convinced that he was right, and so persuasive, that eventually we agreed with him.

Meanwhile, the news about men being taken forcefully from their houses was spreading, while entire families tried to discover their fate in vain. Men left their homes less often. People organized hiding places, usually in attics and basements where they hid men in emergencies. We did it as well. We concealed part of the attic and when the news about men being taken or about incidents in the streets increased, we hid Father and Sierioża.

Today, in hindsight, it seems childishly naïve.

But still it happened in those unpredictable times that such simple manoeuvres or incidents saved lives. In a pre-ghetto incident, my friend's father and brother were taken. My friend stayed behind with her mother and 15-year-old nephew, who had stood behind the half-open door the whole time the Nazis were plundering the house. He managed to survive the war.

In our case, the Gestapo turned up not in the night but during the day. The officers asked about a radio. It stood plainly visible in the dining room. Father pointed at it.

"Don't play the fool. I'm asking about the broadcasting equipment," snapped the German.

"We have no broadcasting equipment," replied father.

"Well, let's get dressed then," he commanded, pointing at Father and my husband. "You too," he looked at the women, "get out!"

We all left the apartment.

One of them locked and sealed the door.

The other two started to walk down the stairs when a third one called out to them:

"Dort blieb ein shones, weisses Katzchen, es wird doch Hunger leiden[3]," he ripped the seal and opened the door. He told us to find our adorable white angora cat Wasylisa and to take her with us.

"Na, raus[4]," – he finished the incident.

We left our house. On the street, the older one pointed at Sierioża:

"Du ghest mit uns. Ihr seit frei."[5] He nodded towards us, the women.

They left. We returned to the house, to Auntie Ola's flat.

That day many men were taken from their homes, amongst them Mr. M. Cukierman, a producer and owner of the medical equipment shop where Mom got supplies for her practice, doctor Wygodzki, a well-known doctor and philanthropist, and many others in Vilnius.

The women who'd been left behind ran from home to home, asking one another if they knew where their fathers, husbands, sons and brothers had been taken. But no one had any knowledge to impart. Some of them summoned the courage to go to the Gestapo to ask about their men. Soon enough, they stopped trying as all they were met with was dismissal. Some snuck up to the Gestapo building, waited for the patrolling guard to reach the other end of the building, then approached the basement windows and uttered the names of their loved ones. No one replied. Sometimes if the windows were open a crack, they threw in some bread – just in case.

Just like the other women, we knew nothing about Father's or Sierioża's fate. It's still hard to think about those dreadful days.

After about a week or ten days, when we were beginning to lose hope that we would ever see them again, a Gestapo officer unsealed and unlocked the apartment, pushed Father inside and told him to think hard about where the broadcasting equipment was, then left.

---

3   "A pretty white kitten remained there, but it will suffer from hunger."
4   "Well, out" (German)
5   "You are coming with us. You are free." (German)

When Father walked into Auntie Ola's apartment we couldn't believe our own eyes. After a few seconds of stunned silence, Mom ran towards him, hugged him and held him tight like she wanted to keep him forever with her, weeping for a long time on his chest, unable to utter a word.

Father was changed beyond recognition. Unshaven, with deep lines around his mouth, filthy and hungry, his eyes sunken and empty. He seemed to be indifferent to everything around him. After those first confusing moments, once he'd cleaned himself up, shaved, and put on pyjamas, we could see how much weight he'd lost. Mom gave him tea with a roll of bread but didn't really encourage him to eat – she was afraid of digestive issues after a period of starvation. He looked at us with his unseeing eyes and stroked our faces with his warm, gentle hands.

A few hours passed before we began to talk. Our first questions were obviously about Sierioża. But Father could not tell us anything about him. He thought he was going to see him at home. They'd been together until they were taken to the dark underground Gestapo corridor. There they were separated, and he hadn't been able to find out anything about him since then. He was pushed into a cell, overcrowded and full to bursting. It was half-lit, airless and crammed. Men stood, sat or lay down on the floor, unable to change positions without cooperation from the others. There were all sorts of people – educated and uneducated, wealthy and poor – but all were guilty of only one crime: Jude[6]. no one had been interviewed, asked anything or told why they were there or what would happen to them. Once a day they were given a cup of cold water and a piece of bread.

One day, they called Father out of the cell and everyone was sure it was the beginning of the end for all of them.

But the Gestapo officer took him home.

Soon, it turned out that the German management of the Kurlandzka oil mill had requested Father's release for they were having difficulties carrying out their technical tasks.

We never found out anything about Sierioża. Until they began locking

---

6   "Jew" (German)

Jews in the ghetto we made every effort to find out where he was, to send him messages, food, clothes, to get word from him or about him. Rózia and I made endless contact with people who promised us the world. We gave away more and more valuables, handing them out right and left to countless fraudsters who popped up along our path like mushrooms. Everyone had a thread that eventually led nowhere. Every day, we returned exhausted by this constant battle between hope and despair, humiliated by another cheater.

On the 6th of September 1941, the day they locked up the ghetto, I came back home around noon and found my parents looking very anxious.

"Dr. Długi telephoned," Father informed me. "He said that he had some news from a reliable source that today at 1pm they will lock the Jewish district. Our house will probably be inside the ghetto. He advised us to leave home earlier if we still want to follow our plan. What do you think?"

"We decided a long time ago what to do in such a situation." I replied.

"Then we have no time to lose. But where is Rózia?"

"I don't know, she hasn't come back yet. She should be here any minute."

"We can't leave with any suitcases or packages. There are lots of Germans walking around," said Father. Mom and I prepared a "package" for each of us. in each there was a change of underwear, a nightgown, soap, a towel and toothbrush. We split the cash we had at home into four parts so each of us would have our own lot in case we were separated. It wasn't much. But what more could we do?

"We can't all wait for Rózia," I said. "You go and I will wait. It won't make much sense for all four of us to leave together at the last minute."

I begged my parents and they left. Rózia barged in, breathless, at 12.45 exactly. It was the kind of detail you remember forever.

"What's happened? Where are your parents?" She asked anxiously, already getting a sense of the atmosphere on the street.

"I'll tell you later. We need to leave home immediately. Here is your bag and money. Follow me."

We got out. The streets were full of nervous people moving fast. We were surrounded by petrified eyes. Everyone was in a hurry, racing towards destinations only they knew of. A strange silence befell this very intense movement. People barely talked to each other, and if they did, it was in half-whispers. The uniformed Germans walked impassively through the crowd. Only they knew what was coming.

Without much difficulty, we reached the agreed-upon location. Mr. Stanisław Frąckiewicz (coincidently, we met three Frąckiewiczs with big hearts on our way), received us kindly as if it was completely natural that we had come to his place. He lived in a house with his wife and a son who had mobility issues caused from polio he had contracted in childhood. He showed us to our room, fed us and gave us a drink. We were able to unwind a bit. Nature and stillness surrounded us. Two or three days passed by like this. We hadn't yet processed the situation; we didn't have or try to make any plans for the future. We were in a state of innocent bliss, happy with our first success – avoiding the ghetto.

However, our future plans were decided for us.

"They are going to herd Jews from other districts to the ghetto in the coming days," Mr. Frąckiewicz brought news from the city.

"They've announced the death penalty for hiding Jews," he said another time.

Anxiety and tension set in. Mr. Frąckiewicz became more subdued and grim, his wife increasingly more anxious. It became clear that this stopover would not last long.

"Rumor has it that the Germans are going to search our neighborhood. They are going to look for Jews in our houses soon," Mr. Frąckiewicz brought more bad news from his neighbor.

"We are leaving Vilnius," responded Father. "Don't be nervous, Mr. Frąckiewicz."

"I'm not afraid, but my wife is very scared. You understand, engineer. She is scared mainly for our son," came his reply.

"I understand, Mr. Frąckiewicz, and I don't hold it against you. Thank you for what you have done for us."

"But where will you go? Have you got anything arranged?"

"No, we don't, but tomorrow morning we will leave Vilnius. What will be, will be."

The next morning, supplied with food for the first few days, we dressed and put on our armbands and after saying goodbye to our tearful hosts we headed out to the unknown.

We walked along the narrow green streets of the neighborhood unapprehended, until we reached the wide street. The pavements were empty but in the middle of the street a crowd of people was walking slowly – Jews who were being directed to the ghetto. On both sides of this human river, the Germans formed riverbanks. The silence was horrifying. All you could hear was steps. The prisoners' shuffles merged in a fluid murmur with the rhythmically chanted steps of the German escort.

We balked. The only spectators on the pavement. Decorated with our incriminating armbands. We couldn't comprehend what we were seeing with our own eyes. People carried sewing machines, dentist drills, featherbeds, pillows, pushed prams full of things with children's little faces sticking out. Some wore furs, others looked like they'd just popped out for a bit, some were loaded to the breaking point, others had nothing.

I don't know how long we stood in stillness on that empty pavement. The image was imprinted in my memory until I felt I would watch it for the rest of eternity. I cannot understand how, miraculously, no Germans noticed us. Perhaps such an inconsistency was not specified in their orders? Maybe it wasn't part of their duties? Or was it simply a moment of distraction?

A young 19 to 20-year-old boy suddenly appeared in front of us and broke us out of our reverie.

"Engineer Komaj," he said to Father, "why are you standing here with those patches? Take off your coats and run for your lives, this way, straight ahead. The toll house is nearby."

"How do you know me?" asked Father, as though it was important at that moment. The boy named a building site which had been run until recently by Father.

It all took a few minutes. These words of a strange boy pushed us to make a decision, prompted us towards the next step.

Just as we approached the road, Rózia announced that she wasn't going with us.

"I will put your lives at risk with my Semitic face. I have no chance, but you can try. I will try to get through this crowd, go to the ghetto, get back to our apartment. It has lots of food provisions, I will survive until you return," she said.

"We will not be separated. It's bad enough that Sierioża is not with us," replied father firmly. "Either we all go to the ghetto or we leave the city together."

"Then I'm coming with you," decided Rózia.

We took off our coats, folded them over our arms with the armbands concealed, and went in the opposite direction of that endless human stream heading to its fate.

Buildings became scarce. It was a beautiful, autumn day. There wasn't a living soul around us. Fields. If it wasn't for the images hidden under our eyelids of that miserable crowd, you could think that the nightmare was over. However, it was only beginning.

"We will head north-east. Towards Świr, maybe Pastavy. I know lots of people there – Jews and non-Jews – and many people there know me too. We'll find someone who will help us. I built so much over there," said Father.

As soon as we'd passed the toll house, a surprise awaited us. From behind the roadside hill, two 'szaulisi' (Lithuanian police) jumped out at us from nowhere. They signaled to us with their hands to come forward. We had no choice.

"Where are you going?" they interrogated us.

"To Świr," replied Father.

"Świr is quite far," one of them said, like he understood. "What for?"

"We've got family there, it will be easier for us."

"Don't you have family in Vilnius? Are you Jewish?"

"Yes."

"Then you need to come back with us." It sounded like a death sentence.

Apart from Father, none of us women were talking. We stood frozen. But at this moment, I took out of my pocket my share of the money and crammed it into the hand of one of the officers.

"Let us go!" I demanded.

A moment of uncertainty. Then, the one who I'd given the money to turned and said, "Ok, go."

We went our separate ways – they to the city and we – into the unknown.

First Help With Food and Overnight Stays.

Evening fell just as we arrived at a small town whose name I cannot recall. A local pharmacy on the ground floor of a wooden one-story building drew our attention. We decided to go in and ask to stay overnight.

It turned out that the owner was Jewish. The war hadn't reached them yet. A large table covered in a white tablecloth laden with food stood in the center of a dining room under a lampshade.

"I'm an engineer from Vilnius and this is my family," Father introduced us. "Jews in Vilnius have been locked up in the ghetto. We have been walking since the morning. We are looking for somewhere to stay for the night."

"You are welcome," the man replied. "Please, take off your coats. Would you like to freshen up? You can clean yourselves here. And please, sit at the table. We were just about to have supper."

As we ate, we were asked questions about Vilnius. They wanted to know whether many people had left the city, what was happening in the places we'd passed by, what we were planning to do.

"Right now, we're headed for areas where we know people. But we still have a long way to go. Could you please give us a room to stay overnight?" asked Father.

"That might be challenging. I would love to give you a room, but my large family has come from many different places, and I simply don't have any space," he said, apologetic. "Also, I'm not sure what the doctor living above us would think about it..."

We swallowed the last bites of bread with cheese, finished up the warm milk, thanked them and left the house. Obviously, that man did not yet understand what was happening around him.

We left the town on a field path. Our feet were dragging with exhaustion.

A kilometer or two beyond the town, lights started to loom on the left – a village? A farm? And then on the right, out of nowhere, we suddenly noticed a weak little window light. Our instincts told us to be wary of larger clusters and people in wealthy-looking houses. We turned towards the little window on the right.

We came closer and saw a tiny hut with an unkempt thatched roof. We knocked. Inside, we heard shuffling and the voice of an elderly man.

"Who is it?"

"We are from Vilnius. Could you please let us stay overnight?"

The door opened and a small, sleepy old man in a simple linen emerged, unshaven and unkempt just like his hut.

"Well, come in, come in. I live on my own. I don't have much space or comfort but come in. We'll manage somehow."

We walked into the hallway that also served as a barn for a pitiful cow and a pen for a pig. The hard earth floor was covered in dung mixed with leaves. In the light of a candle-end shining from the next room we noticed a few chickens sharing this barn-pen with the cow and the pig. Then he took us into a tiny room. Half of it was occupied by a stove with a bench, on which a sheepskin coat was lying. The rest of the furniture consisted of a table and one chair.

"Please, sit down. I'm far from rich but I have some potatoes. I'll cook them in a minute. There is not much milk left but there should be more in the morning."

We thanked him for the food and asked where we could stretch our legs.

"There is some space upstairs, above the hallway. You will find some hay you can use to sleep on."

We went up the ladder in the hallway to the loft and fell down next to each other on the hay. Exhausted from our journey, we fell asleep immediately, but not for long. First came the fleas, then the mice started emerging from their holes, and finally a cat turned up to hunt. Afterwards the chickens, the cow and the pig woke up. The farmer began his daily routine – started a fire on the stove, shooing the cow away.

When we came downstairs, there was milk on the table and the potatoes were almost ready on the stove. Once they were done, the farmer tipped them onto a towel on the table and invited us to join in – sharing all he had.

The potatoes burnt our fingers. But when washed down with milk they tasted incredible. The farmer asked us nothing.

"What a time to live in!" he kept saying, as though summing up his thoughts.

We thanked him from the bottom of our hearts.

"Well, you go with God. I'm on my own and I have all I need but you don't know where you are going to sleep tomorrow and whether or not you'll have food to eat. Have some bread for the road." The farmer resisted when Father tried to pay him for his kindness. He wiped his hands on his trousers, and then shook hands with each of us and repeated as though trying to reinforce his blessing over us – Go with God.

And so, on we went.

We walked for hours, not meeting anyone, resting briefly, barely talking – because what was there to talk about? We each ate our own piece of blackened bread.

All that we'd been through, the exertion, anxiety and diet of the last few days took their toll – Father had a gallstone attack. The pain overpowered him, and he wasn't able to walk any further. We had to stop our journey. We laid Father down under a roadside tree and, acting like a hot water bottle, we took turns to warm the area of his gallbladder with our hands. It was the only available medicine we had. He was in pain for a long time and even once the pain had passed, he was so exhausted that he couldn't move.

At early dusk we noticed a peasant driving down from the fields on a cart with a horse. When he reached us, we asked if he could give us a lift to the nearby village.

"Why not, sit down. Where are you off to?"

"To Świr."

"You'll get there tomorrow. Do you want to stay overnight in the village?"

"Yes, we would greatly appreciate it."

"You can stay at my house."

Soon we arrived. The housewife brought some hay into a spare room. She even put a small kerosene lamp on the floor. Having kerosene at home was a sign of prosperity at the time.

As we were getting ready to sleep, I noticed that the ribbon on the small pouch hanging on my neck was slightly undone and needed to be fixed.

Each of us had such a pouch on our necks – this also was the result of Mom's experiences from the First World War – we had to guard all our official documents with our life (exam results, diplomas, employment certificates) so when the war was over, we could continue to work. Father even remembered a time during the revolution when he'd bought a herring and realized at home that it was wrapped up in an engineering diploma.

That evening, I secured my documents for "after the war", not realizing that I was sitting just beside a curtainless window.

In the morning, a bit better rested, we set off again on our journey, heading towards a Jewish miller near Świr. Unfortunately, I can't remember his surname. Father had built his watermill some time ago. We arrived at our destination by midday. The miller with his family were there and their watermill worked well. We were welcomed very kindly. They let us freshen up. A table was set up. There was cheese and sour cream, butter, and eggs.

We'd barely sat down to eat when suddenly, two blue-uniformed police officers burst through the door. Without a word, they grabbed Father, arrested him, and took him to Świr.

A few minutes after they left, the miller put on a kaftan, put a bottle of vodka in his pocket and said he was going to Świr.

"I'll have a drink with them at the police station and they will let the engineer go. No point in worrying about it," he said as he left.

The waiting began. Tensions were high. Each hour seemed to last forever. Dusk was approaching. No news.

"I'll go and see what's going on over there," said the miller's son finally, and he left too.

We stayed behind with the women from the miller's family. After a few miserable hours of waiting, we saw the miller's son through the window. Alone. No one moved. No one said a word. Fear gripped our throats. The boy came inside, at leisure.

"It's all right," he said briefly.

"What's all right?"

"Where are they?"

"Why haven't they come back with you?" we flooded him with questions.

"Calm down, calm down. The engineer is in detention and Father is queuing."

"Queuing for what?"

"Well, there are lots of people in detention. Their families come in turn to bring vodka, drink with the police officers and then those in detention are released. They are so drunk that you can barely talk to them, but they keep drinking. Once Father gives them his vodka, they will come back together."

And he was true to his word. They returned that evening. The miller was a bit tipsy, as he'd had to keep up the pretence of drinking whilst topping up the officers' vodka. Father was tired, hunched, with deep lines around his lips that made him look 15 years older.

Later, we'd learn that the peasant who had given us a lift and then let us stay overnight had reported us as escaped communists from Vilnius, claiming that we had some important documents in the pouches that always hung around our necks. He had noticed me securing my pouch through the window.

We spent another day or two with our hosts and Father decided that we would go to Świr where another miller, also a Jew, lived; his electric mill had been built by Father. We would get there and then make a plan for the near future. Evenings fell earlier now and it was getting cooler. We had no warm clothes, no place to stay. How would we survive winter? How to prepare for it? Nagging questions for which we had no answers.

We traveled to the Świrski family in Świr. They had a mill, which had been seized, however it was in working order and they'd gotten something for it. In addition, they had a cow, chickens and all their products, but they weren't stingy about what they owned. They shared readily. They welcomed us kindly and gave us food. There were a lot of runaways from Vilnius and central Poland. The administration and police were Polish just like in Lida – and the Germans estimated that *a divide et impera*[7] approach would be efficient for blowing up lingering tensions between the Poles, Jews, Belarusians, and Lithuanians who lived together in one region. Luckily this approach didn't actually work very well, as after some time fate led us again to Świr, but more about that later.

I don't know why Father decided we would go from Świr to Pastavy, where some years ago, together with the Pergamont family, he had built a small electric power station that served the whole town. Did he naively think that this power station would give us some material resources for survival? In those times? I don't know. Mr. and Mrs. Świrski provided us with food for the journey, paid the fare for the wagon and we went on our way.

---

7   "divide and conquer" (Latin)

Bounty on Father's Head

Soon after we arrived, we learned that the power station had been seized by the occupying forces. Father's associates were struggling to make ends meet.

The news of engineer Komaj and his family's arrival spread through the town like wildfire. It must also have reached the German authorities, because soon, a kind man warned Father that we should hide. Indeed, a few days after we left the Pergamont house, police came for Father. When they realized they'd missed us, they made a public announcement offering a high reward for handing Father to the police station or for providing information about his whereabouts.

And then, something incredible happened. Intimidated, and with the ground shaking under their feet, Jews from the town came together to help us. Every evening after dark, they threw us over fences, plots and bushes from one home to another, ensuring we had somewhere to eat, wash and sleep. It took many days, perhaps more than a week. We were moving slowly towards the town's outskirts, nearing the end of the main road where Father's friend, an old engineer named Jan Hurynowicz, lived in his brick house. He was the uncle of an associate professor and a medical doctor, Janina Hurynowicz, a neurology lecturer at the Stefan Batory University, who in the past had sent Sierioża to Estonia. She had run a neurology clinic in 1939-41 where my husband was her assistant. When the Gestapo had taken him, she had voluntarily attempted to search for Sierioża for a long time. Years later, when I would sometimes go to Vilnius from the village, I used to visit her. It was one of those homes where you could relax mentally, feel like an equal. Even years later, she was still looking for her assistant. I know from her account that Dr. Maria Petrusewiczowa, a gynecologist and the mother of a future minister of navigation, Professor Kazimierz Petrusewicz, also took part in this search. Unfortunately, all their efforts, just like our earlier attempts, were futile.

One evening Father decided to go to engineer Hurynowicz for advice and potential help in getting out of Pastavy. He didn't disappoint us. He received Father, completely disregarded his changed social and economic status, and began right away to consider practical possibilities of getting us out of town. He deemed that it would be the safest to leave the town using a peasant wagon on a trading day during the busiest hours when traffic on the road was heavy, and declared that his house would be the best starting point. He laid out his plan:

"The day before, in the evening, all four of you will arrive at my place. You'll stay overnight and early in the morning you will alight the peasant wagon I will hire and set off towards the trade market in the town." And so it was decided.

Life changed some details, but overall, the endeavor went to plan.

Jews were still protecting us, although the reward was tempting and the death penalty for hiding us was terrifying. Members of the community were informed of our plan and provided Father with old calf-length boots, Rózia with a used sheepskin coat and me with a large wool shawl. Even though it seems unbelievable, still today, after 55 years, I have a jerkin made out of that shawl. It reminds me of those people. I don't know their names or surnames, their fates, probably the worst, but for the past half a century they have stuck in my memory.

On the pre-arranged day, in the evening, "as usual" we went through the hedges to the engineer's house. Blackout was compulsory. Therefore, all windows were tightly covered. Inside it was bright. Father's power station was still working. The table was set, it was pleasantly warm. The ground had already begun to frost. There were two middle-aged women hustling about in the house, shooting us both puzzled and frightened looks, not very willing to talk. The conversation at the table was awkward. What made it even more complicated was the fact that we weren't sure exactly how much the two ladies knew about the plan. The atmosphere became heavy. Engineer Hurynowicz also became more reserved. At one point he excused us and went to the kitchen. We had the sense that they were having a serious conversation about us. We drank our tea in half-silence. Finally, engineer Hurynowicz excused himself again and asked Father to accompany him to the next room. We returned to our sparse chatting and soon, to our great surprise, Father returned and said:

"Well, we've overstayed our welcome. It's time to go." He began to say goodbye to people around the house and, confused, we followed suit.

We left. It was dark and cold. The wind was blowing. Father gave us a sign to stay silent. We held hands – Father was leading us somewhere towards the back of the barnyard. He opened the barn door, used a half-covered torch to somewhat illuminate the space, and guided us to a pile of half-frozen straw. Beside it were some straw mats. We lay down tightly next to each other on the straw to keep warm. Father threw the mats on top of us and then slipped under them with us. After a while, once he was sure that no one was around, he explained to us what had happened. It appeared that the engineer's female cousins (that's what he called them) had sensed that something dodgy was going on and announced that they refused to take part in something that would put their lives at risk. Engineer Hurynowicz had explained to them that nothing untoward was going on and that their visitor was genuinely his Jewish colleague who is also an engineer from Vilnius, and it would be simply rude not to invite him and his family for supper. Afterwards, he'd taken father aside to apologize, and informed him that he would not be able to invite us to stay overnight as had been the plan. Nevertheless, he'd told Father where we could survive the night, and then said goodbye to us.

We were very cold that night. The temperature was a few degrees below zero, frost covered everything, and the wind blew mercilessly through the gaps in the timber walls of the empty barn.

In the early morning a peasant wagon pulled up. I think that the ladies were still sleeping, but the engineer came out on the veranda to take a look at his property and land. He avoided making any gesture towards us, let alone a word, but his look was enough to say goodbye.

With a letter from a Pastavy Jew to his friend in Łyntupy in hand, we went to the city market and from there we used the same wagon to Łyntupy. Our guide took a long time at the market and as a result we had to spend the night on the road. It just so happened that the overnight stay was in a village, or a settlement called Komaje. Before then I had never met any person with this name or any place with a similar sound and I knew that Father came from the Kharkov region in Ukraine.

"I'm guessing there must be some connection with this settlement," said Father when I asked if the strange coincidence reminded him of something.

Circumstances didn't allow us to continue our conversation – we weren't alone.

We stayed at our guide's godfather's house, a fairly wealthy peasant for the time, whose welfare was evidenced by a wooden floor, a large "showroom" with two beds and piles of pillows in starched cases, reaching almost to the ceiling – from the biggest to smallest – and tucked in corners. We slept in beds – Mom with Father and me with Różka. What a luxury!

They were very hospitable, fed us in the evening and morning and just before noon we got to Łyntupy.

In Łyntupy, the Priest and the Rabbi Lived in One Place.

It was a small town located near the pre-war Polish-Lithuanian border, inhabited by Belarusians, Jews, Poles and Lithuanians – but from the lifestyle and the look of it, it felt like it was a much larger village.

We arrived in front of a one-story house, having left Pastavy with an address and a letter vouching for us. The addressee turned out to be a local rabbi. The building housed two homes – In the right wing was the apartment of a young rabbi in his thirties. He lived with his wife and a few children. In the left wing lived a local priest who was approximately the same age as the rabbi. We found out later that they collaborated to help runways who were being persecuted for various reasons and were hiding in the area. After a brief deliberation by the priest and the rabbi, we were "referred" to a place with bed and board that belonged to a Jewish lady who owned a fabric shop. Father was meant to report to the rabbi a few days later to "complete the formalities".

The fabric shop was in the main market in a one-story house, common for this town. The veranda opened straight into a room where there was a large stove with a place to sleep on top; windowless, it was lit only by the light coming through the glass in the door. From there, one door on the right led to the shop and another on the left to an apartment which consisted of three small rooms with windows facing the market. We were assigned the first one, which held a sofa where my parents slept and a table on which Rózia and I slept together. The next room was rarely used for anything, and the shop and house owner resided in the third one. There were three people in the family - a mother and two unmarried women. I don't know what illness the elderly woman suffered from, but she was always lying down in her room on a high bed with pillows. From her very own "throne" she called her daughters one by one and commanded them audibly in a loud, cracked voice. All this oscillating activity, including changing the chamber pot, was carried out through our room; it was rarer during the night as at that time she only had one task for her daughters. A few times a night you could hear her loud voice: "kakn, kakn, kakn, kakn..."[8] – in translation: sh.., sh.., sh.. Then a sleepy voice of one of the daughters carried through the two rooms separating us: "bald, bald, bald..." (in a minute, in a minute). We would hear sounds from the kitchen, the voices of the sleepy daughters arguing about whose turn it was this time, then heavy breathing, bare feet stamping, the old woman urging loudly. One of the daughters would pass through our room in her nightdress, her braided hair unkempt, holding a chamber pot in front of her. Then we would hear heavy, labored breathing, reciprocal insults, the old woman's decisive commands about what to do and how, a moment of silence and finally the unmistakable sounds of the woman relieving herself. The olfactory result of this action would reach us later as the daughter passed us by on her return journey. This was repeated a few times during the night. During the day, things were similar but with a slight difference, as the daughters had to go to the shop so there were no arguments about whose turn it was to do what. Apart from these typical nightly tasks, other duties had to be done: cleaning, Mother's morning washing and dressing, cooking and above all taking care of the "pornose" (earnings) in the shop.

It was half-dark everywhere during the day. Through the window we looked out on an empty, sleepy little square. It was as though life had stopped here; news of the shocking historic events unfolding nearby had barely trickled in. If it wasn't for the thoughts racing through our heads about what to do next, we might have had a moment of respite after our Świr-Pastavy "adventures." I don't know whether those two tired old spinsters received

---

8   "shit" (Yiddish)

compensation for our stay from anyone. After all, there were four of us and they fed and cared for us. If they were paid, from which resources had the compensation come? Perhaps it was a Jewish community which was still functioning and untouched in this part of the world? Perhaps it was some sort of priest-rabbi fund? The cash we had taken from home was dwindling. We knew we had to find some way to be needed so we could earn our board and lodging. But at the same time using us as a workforce game with grave risks. Who would have the courage to employ us? Our only "sedative" was Father. Since he was an incurable optimist in character, even in the darkest of times he could always muster up a joke or a prank, but above all the love and warmth he showered on us were like an amazing and endless wellspring of medicine. This added to our strength. After a few days, Father went to the rabbi to "take care of the formalities" which meant that we had to register our residency, but we had no proof of identity. We'd destroyed our identity cards when we'd left Vilnius for on them was clearly written: Jewish nationality. We only had our professional certificates. In Łyntupy, we acquired some certificates which could be used for registering our residency. They also confirmed that we were Jews, however the priest and rabbi thought that it would be better for us to have these papers than none.

There was no way we could find any employment in Łyntupy or its surroundings. The necessity of taking to the road again began to grow, but not before a few weeks and many long days which gave us an opportunity to talk to Father about Komaje, our "namesake" village, which had taken us in for one night on our way from Pastavy to Łyntupy. And it went like this:

Father came from the Jewish town of Bykowo in Ukraine. His name was Don. In Russian he was called Don Jakowlewicz, which made it clear that my grandfather's name was Jakow which means Jakub. But in my father's papers – his father's name was Orel, which I only found out in Lyntupy. Where did this discrepancy come from? As it turned out, my father was born in the previously mentioned Bykowo but his father, my grandfather, had come to Bykowo from Lithuania, where my great-grandfather lived with his many children. Two of his sons who were close in age were called Orel and Jakub.

I think compulsory military service at the time lasted for 25 years. Lots of people managed to avoid it. When Jakub reached recruitment age, Orel had just passed away from tuberculosis, which was raging wildly at that time and decimating people in towns and villages. My great-grandfather cleverly decided to combine two disasters into one. He buried Orel under the name Jakub, and the real Jakub, my grandfather, was sent with Orel's papers to Ukraine, where he settled in the town of Bykowo, in the Kharkow region, and kept the name Jakub in his daily life. Of his father's twelve children, nine died of tuberculosis in Bykowo. Only the three children who left the town early enough survived – my father, his oldest sister Zina, who married a man from Dniepropietrowsko (formerly Jekatierinoslaw), and his oldest brother, uncle Iliusza, who went to Kiev where he obtained qualifications as an accountant, got married and settled. Uncle Iliusza let my father stay with him in Kiev during his studies, but was sadly murdered by Nazis in the courtyard in front of his home. Komaje was probably the place where my great-grandfather made the brave decision to bury a "living" son so as to keep alive the son who'd "died," getting him out of serving in the tsarist army.

After this brief digression, I return to our situation in Łyntupy.

It was becoming clear that despite people's kindness, we would not be able to stay long in Łyntupy. None of us could do any work there.

We set off once more on our journey. This led us again to Świr. In the meantime, winter came, and snow began to fall. The peasants replaced their wagons with sledges. We bid our hosts, the priest and the rabbi, farewell. They gave us a sledge on which to get to Świr and an official (albeit falsified) referral for Father to work in Świr, issued by a town mayor, whom we had never even seen with our own eyes.

Świr, a Second and Final time.

It was a beautiful, sunny, winter day. A gorgeous old forest with heavy snow-capped trees stretched out on both sides of the road. The only sound in the otherwise eerie silence was that of the gently squeaking sledges. Once, a journey in such scenery would have made us very happy – on that day, it didn't give us any enjoyment but rather sadness, making us aware of the contrast between this beautiful day and what was happening with us and around us.

Our journey to Świr went smoothly and we stayed once again with the good Świrski family.

Świr had changed a lot during the few weeks of our absence. A wave of runaways had flooded the town and it had become very crowded. It was difficult to find a roof to shelter under. From dawn to dusk, the main street was full of people with anxious, restless eyes who looked incredibly sad. Everyone was in a constant hurry, people were coming and going, conversing frantically and trading wares to buy food. Friends and relatives would unexpectedly meet in this little town and hug with tears of joy, or pain if the meeting brought news about the loss of loved ones. The new mayor in town had a reputation for being a just man. People said that nobody had known him before and that he was probably a runaway from central Poland himself. He spoke fluent German and in contrast to the local population, he spoke Polish as well.

Mr. Świrski advised Father to go to the mayor and ask for employment as a specialist. Father was hesitant – he wasn't sure he wanted to be dependent on the authorities. Perhaps he was even afraid of refusal? He was also constantly preoccupied with the fact that he could not for the life of him recall the name of an old miller whose mill he had once built somewhere beyond Świr, in the woodland. He nurtured an almost a superstitious belief that if he could get in touch with him, he would get some help. The mill was in a remote area. Father knew that the miller used to come to Świr to run errands and to sort out official matters, so it seemed to him that he would eventually meet him one day in Świr.

And that's exactly what happened. So, for some time, our fate intertwined with this man's.

I still don't know what his real name was. He was known by the nickname Kiezik in the distant areas surrounding his mill. (I guess that in the local dialect it meant 'Kozik,' a large penknife in a leather cover. But why exactly Kiezik – I don't know.)

At that time, he was an older man, slender, very tall, slightly slouched, and had grey hair and a charming demeanor. He recognized Father on the street immediately. When he heard of our situation, he was concerned and stated straight away:

"I've got enough space and bread. If necessary, engineer Komaj (that's what he called Father), bring your women and come – we'll survive one way or another. Don't worry, engineer Komaj, it's not charity. If you can fix or build something for me, it will be worth the price of staying at my place in the village."

However, after discussing it with Świrski and Kiezik, it was decided that Father should go to the mayor first and see what he could offer. If nothing came of it, Father would ask to be referred to Kiezik as a technical supervisor. If necessary, Kiezik was prepared to make an application for his employment. A referral would make not just Father's job legal but also us staying in Świr at all. It was worth the risk.

The mayor received Father kindly and with respect. He said that he would try to arrange something and asked him to come back in a few days.

"I've made an arrangement for you," the mayor said without preamble when Father returned the second time. "I'll employ you as a technical supervisor for the mill in Świr and its surrounding areas. I am having trouble with flour for bread; so many people come over here but every now and then a mill is out of order. Here you go, this is an employment order, a technical inspection of the mills order, a list of the mills, allocation of a house to live in, "Aryan" food stamps (these were slightly larger portions), and," he added quietly like he was explaining himself "it wasn't me who divided people, food stamps and fuel allowance according to their race."

We listened to Father's account of his visit to the mayor with disbelief, as if it were a fairy tale.

"The mayor is strange," Father remarked pensively.

His name was Leon Świechowski. His manner and fluency in German and Polish suggested that he didn't come from the Eastern Borderlands.

Later on, we heard that he was a Jew, an escapee from central Poland, a journalist. How much truth there was in the rumor, I have no idea.

The house we were given turned out to be built with red bricks. It contained two rooms - a kitchen with an electric light and an oven. It was located at the end of the main street, beyond the most populated Jewish area but just across the street from it. Father registered his and our food stamps. His spirit was lifted knowing that he would work and be occupied with things he knew and liked. Generally speaking, he was a true workaholic, especially when it came to his profession, even in those times. Besides, Mom was the same.

It seemed that we had achieved a bit of stability in a reality that was ever-shifting. This lasted only a few months, but during that time lots of people came and went through our home on their journey.

I think that Szmerka Kaczergiński turned up first – a Jewish journalist and poet whom I knew from my time as a student, from our hiking trips through woodlands, around the beautiful lakes and Neris riverbanks. We were a joyful, friendly, singing and carefree crew. Therefore, our meeting, despite changes in circumstance, was very happy, full of stories about our fortunes, but also full of memories. He spent a few days at our place and told us about his war story up to that point.

He still had the same light blue eyes, full of mischievous sparkle which made him good looking – and this was an advantage in his situation. On the other hand, his Polish was poor, even for someone from the Eastern Borderlands – and that was a problem. To decrease suspicion of him, thanks to the urging of Mrs. Wiktoria Grzmielewska (Mrs. Wika), he became a fake mute. This process was very difficult for him – he had to learn to live without talking. He practiced it when he was in Vilnius and lived at Mrs. and Mr. Maria and Feliks Wolski, where Mrs. Wika lived as well. His main job was to go shopping at the market. Mrs. Wika often accompanied him, and sometimes Felek did too if the shopping was heavy.

Mr. and Mrs. Wolski's apartment was a place where various "suspicious" people with the "wrong" look, race, views, and activities met. You could come over to feel freer, to see kind faces, seek advice, get help, but also just to eat a bowl of hot soup. Every time I went there, a pot of soup was waiting in a windowless kitchen for visitors.

Mrs. Maryla and Mr. Felek lived at 16 Wielka Pohulanka on the top floor. There was only a loft above their apartment, which was never locked, all throughout the occupation. A nearby Jewish Scientific Institute (IWO) was ordered to be destroyed. The order was meant to be carried out by Jews, who were brought over in a working crew from the ghetto specially to do this job. Among them were people who were aware of the cultural value of the items featured at IWO, and they made efforts and took risks to save at least some of these treasures. Some Poles, including the Wolski family, helped them with this endeavor.

Mr. Felek told me once that anyone interested in saving valuables knew that the loft in their house could be used. They made good use of this opportunity. One day, a group of workers without armbands brought two chests on a two-wheeled barrow and put them in a discreet place in the loft. Szmerka Kaczergiński and a lawyer, Mietek Zaborowski, were involved.

The chests survived the entire war up in the loft. They even had their own interesting story as for some time they were used as a bed by a Jewish couple – friends of the Wolskis – who were hiding in the loft. According to

Mr. Felek, the chests contained files, catalogues, manuscripts, old prints and also a bust sculpture made by Marek A. Antokolski.

Kaczergiński, who had been trained to be mute, wound up as a farmhand at an estate near Świr. He told us that the estate was run by an old, crazy, temperamental and bossy heiress. She was fond of the new helper and gave him many orders, which meant that he spent more time in the rooms than other servants. It became almost idyllic. Until a day came when her helper could no longer take the heiress' demands and whims.

"For fuck's sake, what do you want?!" Szmerka couldn't hold it together any longer when she kept changing her mind and spoke through clenched teeth.

The heiress didn't even hear the end of the sentence, since she had fainted from fear after hearing the voice of her mute servant. Szmerka was equally scared, but didn't faint, only jumped out of the window and escaped to nearby Świr.

Everyone who arrived at Świr asked around on the streets about people from their town. That's how Szmerka found us. He spent a few days, maybe a week with us. He didn't plan to stay in a large Jewish population, he wanted to travel further away.

At the same time, a son of my parents' friends turned up – Jerzyk Bazylian. He was ten or eleven years old. His parents had died in the Vilnius ghetto, but he'd escaped and had come to Świr on his own. He had a very pleasant face, grey eyes with beautiful long eyelashes, and he spoke Polish very well. His mother was from Warsaw. Even though there were many differences between Szmerka and Jerzyk, who were different ages and came from completely different communities (Szmerka from a family of Yiddish-speaking, popular Vilnius academics, and Jerzyk from a Polish-speaking, assimilated, middle-class family), they were somehow drawn to each other and had a lot to talk about. When they talked (we didn't know yet what about) in a corner, you could see a similarity between them – in their facial expression, their eyes.

It was obvious to us that this kid who'd found us, friends of his parents, would stay with us for better or worse. However, children in those times grew up very quickly. We were incredibly surprised when Jerzyk announced that he would go with Szmerka – even though he didn't know where they would be going. Szmerka encouraged it. We didn't dare dissuade him from his decision as we didn't know whether we could secure a better fate for him than Szmerka. Besides, they had already made their choice. After a short stay, they headed out and we never heard from them again. Only after the war did I receive a message that Szmerka had survived the occupation only to die in a French plane crash. I've never heard anything about Jerzyk. I'm not even sure whether they were together for a long time or soon went their separate ways.

In Świr, Jula lived with us for some time. She was Polish, a communist from Białystok and it was the second time she had appeared in our lives. She came to us the first time right after the German-Soviet war broke out in 1941 and another wave of runaways arrived in Vilnius, this time from Białystok. She came with a message from my friend from university, Dina Druskinowna from Białystok, who asked me to help Jula however I could. She stayed with us. I can't remember where she was when we left our home.

When we were at the miller's house near Świr, the memory of Father's arrest came to me. We were all sitting frozen around the table. Nobody said a word, including Jula, but she did eat a whole bowl of cheese with sour cream. She told me later that her usual reaction to stress had always been hunger. This scene stuck in my memory as some sort of *curiosum*[9]. She didn't take part in our journey to Pastavy and Łyntupy.

The second time our paths crossed was when she lived with us in Świr, although she often went off on her own. She went to Vilnius a few times, helping to put separated family members in touch with one another, handed out messages, perhaps brought some food, perhaps this was her way of earning money? I do not know. For one of her trips, Mom asked her to find out some information about her large family in Vilnius, particularly about her two sisters, their husbands and children. We gave her the address of our former housekeeper Emilia, who lived on Mała Stefańska street, close to the ghetto. If she could manage to get in touch with someone from the ghetto, our flat was meant to be occupied by my best friend from school, Masza

---

9   "curiosity" (Latin)

Bialer. After a short time, Jula came back with news and with an older man, a pharmacist who had escaped from the ghetto.

Jula told us that no one from Mom's family had survived, that one night the Nazis took two thousand people from the ghetto, herded them to Ponary, told them to dig ditches and then shot them there so their bodies would fall into the ditches. Mom's closest family was amongst them.

We were aware of the difficult conditions in the ghetto, the lack of space, starvation, spreading diseases, and backbreaking slave labor, the random shootings. But this was the first we'd heard about systematic mass massacring of random people. We were all shocked and Mom just couldn't believe it.

"This is some delirious and sick imagination. I understand, it's a war, people die, even bystanders, but this, what Jula is telling us, it's impossible. Surely the Germans are cultured and civilized people. How can you believe such nonsense?" Mom said quietly when Jula went out to the other room.

Jula's trip also brought information that Masza, who was still alive, was living in my room and had sent out lots of our family photos. Later, Masza Bialer froze to death on the way from Stutthof (the camp near Gdansk) to Białystok as the camp was being liberated. But all our photographs survived the war and I still have them.

Every time I return to this treasure, I remember Masza and her sad life.

Her mother had died of tuberculosis when Masza was a young child. Soon after, her father married his deceased wife's sister, per the common custom amongst Jews which had the child's welfare in mind. The auntie-stepmother was a good person and her relationship with her niece-stepdaughter was incredibly warm. Their connection became even deeper after the death of the auntie's twelve-year-old daughter, whom she'd had with Masza's Father.

After the occupation I crossed paths with Masza's auntie, Mrs. Berta Bialerowa.

The pharmacist brought over by Jula turned out to be a drug addict. A few times a day he became very dejected and was in a state of drowsiness he couldn't overcome. I thought it was a result of starvation or exhaustion from recent experiences (leaving the ghetto, the journey to Świr). It was strange that in such a state he found it very difficult to motivate himself, but then he would go out to another room and return after a short while animated and ready to talk. When I shared my observations with Mom, she explained what was going on.

"Take notice," she said, "he has marks from the needle on his arms where he injects the drugs."

It was one of those short lessons of medical observation I casually received here and there from Mom.

The owner of a small yet elegant shop selling women's accessories on Wielka Street in Vilnius also called at our place in Świr. She looked good and spoke well and could sew. She'd been wandering around in the area, from village to village. In each village she stayed for some time as she sewed for anyone she could and then when she was recommended by her clients, moved to another village. She had bed and board. She spent some two days with us and went on.

The pharmacist also made some arrangements somewhere. I think he had money. Lots of other people I didn't know or can't remember rolled through our house.

The three of us women ran the house and "received the visitors." Father spent a lot of time out. He visited the mills – fixing, advising, altering. When he returned from his trips, he sometimes brought some lard, other times it was chicken, grains, flour, potatoes, some vegetables, eggs. We had enough food, were able to feed this person and that, sometimes even to provide them for their journey. But Mom was still very depressed and lived in constant fear, mainly for Father's life.

When he was out, she was scared that the worst would happen to him somewhere – and when he was at home that one day fate would come knocking at the door. Only in the moments of his return would her grey eyes brighten with joy and unconditional love for him.

Rózia was consumed by a guilty conscience that she was constantly endangering us with her Semitic looks. The lack of any information about her family in Łódź and Bucharest or about her brother, my husband, caused her considerable pain. She quickly gave up on any news ever coming of them.

During his time at home, Father often remarked that perhaps we needed to move to a less populated area, somewhere off the beaten path. Sometimes he would observe that we might be forced to do it and said that he'd spoken to people he trusted about such matters. These vague remarks made me think that I should learn some farm work just in case. This led to me training with Mrs. Świrska. I was hastily taught to milk a cow, care for chickens, bake bread, and manage milk - which included storing cream, making cheese, cottage cheese, even butter. Soon these skills would come in handy.

One day, a rumor spread around Świr that a Latvian punitive and pacification squad was heading toward us. Jews called them "hundert achzige" which roughly meant the "hundred and eighty ones" – men had to be one hundred and eighty centimeters tall to be accepted into the unit. They were known for their horrific cruelty.

Within a few hours, panic set in throughout the whole town. Scarce goods disappeared from the shabby stalls. Traffic intensified on the main street. Everyone was in a hurry, buying and selling things to and from each other. The demand for bags, strong strings and straps increased – they were needed for improvised backpacks. You could see increasing anxiety in people's eyes and movements. A popular idea was to run away from town. People were "packing up" – they bound duvets and pillows, attached pots and mugs to them, put on as many layers of clothing as they could. The exodus began at dawn – a mass of people escaped through the frozen Świrski lake to the forest on the opposite bank. Some individuals and small groups split up from the main crowd and took different routes – seeking help from peasants they had befriended in nearby villages.

Father wasn't in Świr, he was visiting another mill. There were three of us at home – Mom, Różka and me. People came around and urged us to prepare for departure. We were very anxious, but unanimous in our decision – we would not leave home until Father returned or sent a message with instructions for us. We were afraid of losing contact with Father and certain that he would somehow get in touch with us. We sat in a dark room, huddled together and looking through the window. The town slowly emptied out and became quiet. The hours seemed to drag on for eternity as we continued to sit numbly by the window. I was the first to snap out of this state.

"Maybe there's a way to find out what's happening," I suggested.

"But how, where? This late at night?" they objected.

"I could try to get through to the mayor, to his house."

"Are you kidding? He doesn't have to receive Jews at night. It's bad enough what he has to deal with now that they're in the city hall. He has already done as much as he can," they tried to discourage me from my initiative.

We knew that the mayor lived closed by, on the next street in a small, inconspicuous house. It was situated in a way that it could be reached by going through the fences, without needing to access the main road.

"I'll go," I insisted. "He might know where Father is. Perhaps he could advise us?"

They gave in.

I went out into the electric stillness, treading cautiously, barely breathing. There was complete stillness around me. Every now and then a dog would bark slightly and briefly, like even it knew that it was an evening to be quiet and to ignore anybody who was sneaking about. I went through a few yards and gardens and knocked on the door. I heard steps approaching inside.

"I'll be with you in a minute," a quiet, female voice informed me without asking my name and the door opened, revealing a dark hall. "Please, come in," the voice urged. She was barely recognizable in the darkness.

Once the front door had shut behind me and the door to the room was opened, I could see in the light of a kerosene lamp a young, elegant woman, probably in her thirties. She stood in a tidy large room which contained some holy picture, a few starched serviettes, plant pots, a tapestry hanging above the sofa and the strangest part of all, a small, clean, young white goat who wouldn't leave its owner's side for a moment.

"Who are you?" she asked, taken aback.

"I am the daughter of engineer Komaj. The name probably means nothing to you. I wanted to get some advice from the mayor about what we should do. I thought that maybe he would know where my father is."

It seemed to me that for a split second I saw fear, hesitancy or uncertainty in her eyes. However, she quickly collected herself and spoke in the quiet, calm voice I'd heard before:

"My husband is not at home. He has not returned yet. The town is so unsettled. When I opened the door for you, I was sure it was him returning."

She stopped for a moment, as if her thoughts had suddenly broken off and were running on an invisible trail after her husband.

"I know about your family," she finally went on, "but I don't know how to advise you. The town is so unsettled," she repeated and her tone made it clear she was worried about staying here. "If I were you, I think I would wait for contact with your father, but I'm not sure if I can officially advise you."

We said goodbye, she shook my hand kindly and let me out, making sure that the light did not shine outside.

I went home. All we could do was wait.

I'm not sure how much time passed until we heard a sledge squeaking very softly on the snow. A man shook off a hooded greatcoat and walked slowly towards the entrance to our house. It wasn't Father. Barely breathing, we dreaded to imagine what would come next.

Was it bad news about Father? Was it someone with bad intentions towards us? Would they take us away? Torture us? Bad thoughts raced through our minds.

But it was simply old Kiezik.

"Praise be to God," he greeted us. "I see all three of you are healthy and in one piece. Come on, get dressed, take whatever you have, I'll take you to my village."

"What about Father?" we protested.

"What about him? He is at my place. He wanted to come here, but I wouldn't allow it. There is enough misfortune going around. One doesn't need to seek it out."

Dear Kiezik

At the Ranger Station

Just like the well-known proverb states "all roads lead to Rome," in our case for some time they invariably led to Kiezik. Many wonderful people were part of our experiences in the Belarusian countryside and Kiezik was a central fixture in them.

We went off to the countryside. We found out on the way that Kiezik wasn't taking us to his place but to a nearby village, instead. There we were meant to stay in hiding until the trouble abated. Only the farmer, who would provide us with food and change the slop bucket, would know about us.

"We'll see what happens," Kiezik concluded before bidding us farewell.

We arrived at the front yard of the first farmhouse on the edge of a village, the name of which I can't remember. It was still dark. The farmer was waiting, watchful, in the barn. He opened the gate. Without exchanging a word, we were led into a barn full of straw. The farmer took each of us and dragged us into a separate "bunker" in the straw. To this day, its construction remains a mystery to me. The exit was by the barn wall, where the air came in through the gaps in the logs. During the day, you could see a narrow strip of the world, where sometimes dogs ran, sometimes poultry walked by. We were not scared. Kiezik had won our trust and hearts on the spot – we were convinced that all Kiezik's choices and actions were practically infallible and trusted him explicably. Even so, we struggled to manage being separated from Father, whose presence, even in the worst of times, lifted us up and always made us feel happier and warmer.

The separation didn't last too long – for maybe one or two weeks we were completely isolated from the world. We didn't even know the face of our host who looked after us. Ten to twelve days later, Kiezik turned up one night and announced quietly and decisively:

"Come on, we are going to the flat, the engineer is waiting."

After a short journey, we reached a ranger station. Father, a forest ranger, and his wife were waiting for us with a table set and windows tightly covered. It was a moment of pure joy. No one present could ever have suspected that we would live through so many dramatic moments and that Father would still eventually die here. So far, everything was going very well. Above all else, we were together again. Only rarely did someone drop by the ranger station. Even Rózia went out to the forest to breath some fresh air. Father worked every day at Kiezik's nearby mill.

Because Kiezik's mill was subjected to Stara Wilejka administration during the war, Kiezik had procured "papers" which allowed him to employ Father as a mechanic, thus legalizing Father's presence at the mill. Kiezik also provided the forest ranger with flour, hulled grains and sometimes even lard, "so they don't think you're eating their bread for free," as he put it.

Father once told Kiezik that he didn't know how or when he would be able to repay the favor, and Kiezik grunted: "If we stay alive - I will still be in your debt. If it wasn't for you, I might still have my mill, but I wouldn't have anything to eat," and soon he had another task for Father.

This idyll didn't last for long. We began to hear more and more rumors about a blue policeman from Stara Wilejka named Sobolewski roaming around, asking people about Jews hiding in the area. Rumor had it that he kept turning up in neighboring villages. It didn't take long for him to "pay a visit" at the ranger station one evening, finding us unprepared and unable to hide. He arrived by sledge already quite drunk and was accompanied by another policeman, who must have been of a lower rank as he was dutifully following the orders of Sobolewski. Such was the name of the uniformed commander. He stared at us with a drunken and hazy look.

"Come on, give me money!" he stated abruptly.

"We don't have any," Father replied anxiously.

"All Jews have money. No talking. Give me money."

"We don't have any," Father repeated.

"Did you give it all to your hosts?" he questioned.

"We didn't, because we had none."

"In that case, we are going to have a different conversation. Unharness and feed the horse," he barked at his assistant. "And you, hostess, bring us a drink and some food." He sat comfortably at the table. "Everyone, sit at the table, we'll talk differently after some vodka." We hesitated, so he roared, "To the table! Is this your daughter? She sits next to me!" he pointed at me.

We sat down. He poured vodka into the glasses himself as though he was the host. He also poured out a full glass for me.

"Come on beautiful, do you remember now where you are hiding the money?" he turned to me.

"We don't have any money."

"We'll see soon enough. Rip off the wallpaper!" he roared at his assistant. "The bastards have probably papered over it!"

His orders were carried out.

"I didn't find anything," he reported, after thoroughly completing what he'd been ordered to do.

Helpless fury began to grow in Sobolewski. He violently pushed the glass of vodka towards me.

"I said, drink," he spoke through clenched teeth.

I hated vodka and just the smell of it made me feel nauseated. I was stalling.

"For f…k's sake, drink!" he said again, this time unholstering his gun and putting it to my head. "Are you drinking?" he shouted.

"Please miss, drink," the ranger's wife pleaded in a whisper.

I moved the glass closer to my lips.

"Drink, and drink fast! I won't say it again!" I heard.

I drank it all in one go and felt nothing.

"Now talk, where's the money?"

"We don't have any," I said again.

"If you don't have any, you are doomed. Harness the horse! We'll find a place for you in the barn in Stara Wilejka. Get out!"

We had heard of mass executions taking place in Stara Wilejka where barns full of people, mainly Jews, were set on fire.

He ordered my parents to sit in the back and told me and Różka to walk in front of the horse whilst he mounted the sledge next to his assistant with great difficulty. We took to the road, traveling in silence through a beautiful old moonlit forest covered in snow. Sobolewski slept and the horse walked slowly, but Różka and I had to be quick nevertheless to avoid being trampled by the horse. I don't know how long it took.

Suddenly, Sobolewski stopped the horse. I thought he would finish with us in this forest. Why would he drag us with him all the way to Stara Wilejka?

But he had a different idea. He got off the sledge and told Różka to sit in his place, then he dragged me onto the side of the road and walked beside me, pushing me. The forest became less dense. A blurry outline of houses began to loom in front of us. Stara Wilejka?

"You little shit, couldn't you wake me up earlier?" he spoke angrily to his assistant. And to me: "go on, faster!"

We had walked far ahead of the sledge when suddenly he threw me in the snow, his intentions clear. With newfound strength I struggled with him, despite having drunk that glass of vodka and despite the whole horror of that night; it was like those experiences had empowered me in some strange way. And he was very drunk. In the meantime, the sledge caught up with us. Sobolewski got up, fell over in the snow a few times, swore terribly at me, pushed me, then told Różka to get off the sledge, took his seat and we went on. The village was just around the corner.

"Go to the village chief and tell him to feed or change the horse. We'll drink and eat something before we go any further."

The Village Chief of Zahacie

He announced his arrival by kicking the door and roaring: "Open the door!"

Nobody asked: "who is it?" Only a humble voice from behind the door reassured us:

"Just a moment, I'm coming... one moment... one moment..."

We were led into a room with a low ceiling. Instead of floor, the ground was hard earth. An unkempt, sleepy peasant in linen pants and a long shirt was lighting a carbide lamp after making sure that the windows were covered. A woman and a few frightened children who'd been woken up emerged from behind the stove. The youngest, whose bottom was bare, was crying and holding on tightly to his mother's leg. Sobolewski ordered a few things, sat comfortably on a bench, leaned over the table and was soon snoring.

The village chief put on his trousers and a sheepskin coat.

"Woman," he said to his wife, "give them some food and drink, I'll be back in a minute. I'll unharness the horse, feed it and come back, while you give these people some food and drink," he winked at her, knowingly.

The chief's wife pottered around in no hurry. She set out vodka, glasses and some snacks, but she didn't encourage us to eat, and let Sobolewski sleep.

After a little while, the village chief returned, not on his own but in the company of a handsome man with grey hair and a neat beard, dressed in the style of a peasant. The village chief poked Sobolewski. He glanced drunkenly at the visitor and even stood up, though he could barely stay on his feet.

"Sobolewski, what's your business with these people?" the visitor asked him.

"I'm taking them to Wilejka."

"Listen to me, Sobolewski. The Germans won't stay here forever. They will be gone and you'll remember then that Niewiarowicz will be Niewiarowicz again and there won't be any place for you here. I swear it. I advise you to leave these people alone and go on your way."

Imagine our surprise when Sobolewski wobbled on his spread legs, put on his hat, waved his hand at his assistant and left without a word.

We were all numb. The removal of this villain didn't give us a shred of joy.

Father thanked Mr. Niewiarowicz, whom, as it turned out, he knew from some card game meetings. He also thanked the village chief for his common sense, good will, initiative and courage.

"You don't recognize me but I recognized you straight away," the village chief responded to him.

"And how do we know each other?" Father was surprised.

"When you were building a mill in Świr, I came to ask for a job. We were very poor then. The kids were starving. When I told you this, you called a technician and said – give him work, his children are starving. I earned some money, got out of the worst poverty and never forgot you. As soon as I saw you with this drunken scoundrel, I immediately knew – I must rescue them. So I ran to the estate to ask Mr. Niewiarowicz what to do. And he, a good man, dressed up and came with me.

"What are you going to do? We don't have any space and I am constantly under watch as the village chief; otherwise I'd gladly offer you my place."

The village was called Zahacie, but I can't remember the village chief's name.

The only idea we could come up with was to contact Kiezik and seek his help again. Early in the morning, the chief took us to the mill.

Kiezik already knew everything from the forest ranger and was just about to go to Stara Wilejka in an attempt to save us from the hands of our executioners if we were still alive. He had bribes prepared – a goose, vodka and some other things. He was very happy to see us, and his face lit up immediately. It was astonishing – we'd once again barged into his life. It had simply happened.

"That's all right. Freshen up. Eat. Then we'll discuss what to do next."

After breakfast Kiezik laid out his plan:

"It's better not to stay together. You need to separate now. I have already found a space for Różka in the village. I'll hide her well, nobody will know. There is a poor farmer but a good man. He is close by, I'll see to it and give him flour and hulled grains. She can't stay there for free. The engineer has papers – he can stay here at the mill. He'll earn enough money for himself and for you. For the engineer's wife and Pola we need to come up with something else, search for a place. I'll have to talk to someone."

A few days later, Różka went at night with Kiezik to her new "lodgings." I never visited her there. For safety reasons, mainly Kiezik and sometimes Father visited her. While we waited for further arrangements, Father helped Kiezik.

At Nikołaj Aleksandrowicz's

Not long had passed before Kiezik told us that he had found a place for Mom and me.

"I don't know this Łapicki very well myself. But Marianek knows him, he talked to him and he's agreed to take you in. You can rely on Marianek. He said that he would take you over there himself. And the engineer knows Marianek."

"Who is this Marianek?" Mom asked when we were on our own.

"He's a wonderful young man," replied Father.

"How do you know him?"

"I played cards with him once."

"That's all? What else do you know about him?"

"I know he was in a German camp somewhere, escaped and now he works for the Stara Wilejka community and uses his job to help people. He's an amazing man."

Father was naïve and had never been able to read people well, nevertheless I had to admit that he had luck on his side. Mom, on the other hand, was a sceptic. She liked to know everything in detail and to consider all the advantages and disadvantages of a scenario. If she took to someone she was able to trust that person and be a committed friend. Father was very spontaneous in his interactions with others. For that reason, Father's judgment and excitement didn't always sit well with Mom. But our situation was difficult – we had no choice other and one night Mr. Marian arrived at the mill. We said goodbye to Father and Kiezik with heavy hearts and once again we hit the road through the still, majestic forest. The thin snow now was less fluffy and white. It was already April 1942. From the forest we passed onto a lake, still frozen but wet in places. Nobody spoke. Mom was in the back covered with a burka, I was sitting next to Mr. Marian in the front.

Suddenly we heard Mr. Marian's quiet voice, a sound alien in this scenery.

"Miss Pola, are you not afraid? After all, you don't know me nor where I am taking you."

In that moment, a memory of my parents' conversations and Mom's doubts attacked me. I was gripped by fear.

"Mr. Marian, we have no other choice. Come what may." I replied rather calmly.

"Nothing to worry about. I just had this thought, for no reason. I'm sorry." He felt guilty.

"Everything will be alright."

That was the only conversation we held throughout our entire journey.

When we arrived at our destination, the farmer wasn't there. The farm seemed deserted. The house with a thatched roof was low to the ground. A low door and a high doorstep led into a dark hallway. From there, one door on the left led to the farm hand's family room, and the second door on the right – to the farmers' apartment. Here there was a large kitchen with a large stove, then another big room with a wooden floor. Part of the room was separated by a curtain. A hostess emerged from behind the curtain. She slouched, leaning on a walking stick, barely mobile. Her face looked like a mask and she spoke with great effort, straining her words. Mr. Marian seemed to be comfortable there and understood Mrs. Agnieszka very well. She told us to make ourselves at home. Mr. Marian brought warm milk and bread from the kitchen and the atmosphere immediately became more relaxed.

"Do you know what ails her?" Mom asked me quietly at the first opportunity.

"I don't know," I whispered.

"Her condition is typical of Parkinson's disease. Once you've seen it, you will remember it for the rest of your life."

Mom never missed an opportunity to share some knowledge. And not only medical knowledge at that.

The farmer, Nikołaj Aleksandrowicz, returned home a few hours later. He had curly brown hair and a neat beard. He was of medium height, stocky build and he looked strong. His eyes were small, restless and at that moment, glistening. He was a bit tipsy.

"Please ladies, make yourself at home," he welcomed us kindly. "Help yourselves to anything. We'll live together and help each other as much as we can." He spoke in Russian.

Mr. Marian handed him a package from Kiezik.

"The old one has sent you some supplies for now. He says he'll send more later."

He promised to visit us sometimes, said goodbye and went off. We all slept in one room, only Mrs. Agnieszka slept behind her curtain.

In the morning, at dawn, Nikołaj Aleksandrowicz rose quietly, went to the kitchen and began to build a fire. I got dressed and offered to help. He seemed reluctant, but didn't stop me. My efforts were successful. I put on a pot of potatoes with skin for animal feed and another one, with peeled potatoes, for our breakfast. It wasn't easy. The pots had to be placed in the oven using long, quite heavy bars with handles of various sizes for different kinds of pots. If you wanted to see what was happening in the pot, to check if the water had boiled out or something was burning, you would have to take the pot out and add coal to the stove again. If you were clumsy, you could risk the pot overflowing onto the fire and then having to start it all over again. Hot air was blowing through the oven opening which, especially later during the warm summer days, made the job incredibly difficult.

With each day I took on more household duties in the same way I had taken over making the fire. It gave Nikołaj Aleksandrowicz more time for other tasks – fixing the fence, gate and horse mill, running errands in the town. For some time he still milked the cow Basia and fed the pigs until I took on those responsibilities as well.

Mom did lighter work – washing dishes, repairing underwear, sometimes she helped me in the kitchen, supported Mrs. Agnieszka and took her out to get fresh air. When we ran out of bread, I offered to bake it. Nikołaj

Aleksandrowicz had become more confident in my skills. He only advised me to bake it at the farm hand's oven, because it heated up more evenly. The "farm hand" at Nikołaj Aleksandrowicz's farm had not worked for some time, because the farmer couldn't pay him. Every day he went off someplace to earn money. His old mother, whom we called Grandma, stayed at home.

I told Grandma that I wanted to bake bread in her oven. She was actually glad since she was bored being alone at home all the time. I made the leaven and after the appropriate amount of time had passed, I started to knead the dough. It was my first ever performance and I tried my best. Once it was ready, I smoothed its domed surface and made a hollow in the middle so it wouldn't break when rising. At that moment I heard Grandma's voice:

"Why are you making this hollow in the middle like some Jew?"

I explained why I'd done it.

"If you made a cross it wouldn't break either," said Grandma.

For a moment I was speechless.

"Oh, it's simply because it was a Jewish lady who taught me to bake," I came to my senses and explained myself indifferently.

I calmly flattened my "Jewish" hollow and cut a cross on the top of the dough.

This incident, though nerve-wracking, had no consequences. It became Grandma's secret. Did she have any suspicions or associations that she didn't think were worth talking about? Or did she simply believe my explanation? The bread turned out well and nobody doubted my competence in that matter anymore. That was followed by caring for chickens and making dairy – sour milk, cream, cottage cheese, cheese and occasionally butter. I was also going to try to milk Baśka. The cow was calm. She didn't give much milk. She shared the barn with a bull affectionately named Aronczik by Nikołaj. It was a breeding bull that brought income and for that reason was treated kindly by the farmer, even though he could be problematic. He gored this and that person a few times, which complicated relationships with neighbors some. Aronczik was my nuisance. I was scared to go into the barn because of him; the sounds that came out of this enormous black bulk and the wild flash in his eye made me panic.

The living space between Baśka and Aronczik was separated by a bar – I think it was only symbolic. Aronczik was always tied up and it was supposedly safe to go into the barn to milk Baśka, however it took me some time to overcome my fear. At first, Nikołaj came in as well to support me.

There were also piglets, garden patches, two dogs and more. I helped with the farm work; managing the tobacco crop was added to my duties, which required constant work from planting until harvest. The farm was doing better, although Nikołaj Aleksandrowicz and I worked from dawn to dusk. Mom helped as well. Dżok the dog, a German shepherd, led Baśka out to the field and then brought her back, protected the garden from the chickens and the chickens from Amor. Amor was the second dog – a bulldog. If Dżok was hardworking and effective, Amor was the opposite. He was an idle, stupid and malicious lazy-bones. He would sit by the stove the whole day long, snoring loudly and waking up only to eat and cause trouble.

When chickens went into the garden patch, I would shout the order "Dżok-chickens", and Dżok would run along the path between the patches, barking and causing the chickens to flee in a panic. However, I had to remember to close the kitchen door so Amor couldn't get out before shouting the order to Dżok. Once I forgot and the consequences were dire. With uncharacteristic energy, Amor jumped out of the kitchen and ran mercilessly over the garden patches. He chased the chickens, catching one by its tail, and locked his jaws – which was normal for this type of breed. Luckily the chicken managed to escape, although without its tail. Amor ran around for a little while with feathers sticking out of his muzzle, looking like he had a strange moustache. The chicken had a bare bottom till the end of its life and from that day on I always remembered to close the door. I didn't like Amor, I was scared of him.

By contrast, Dżok was the first dog I loved and he felt it. He sat next to me during meals, put his muzzle on my lap and waited patiently until I gave him something to eat. He never reached for anything on the table or nudged me, he was very well-behaved. Still, he preferred to go around the farm and to the fields with Nikołaj Aleksandrowicz. At night, Dżok stayed outside and guarded the farm.

One day, early in the morning, Nikołaj realized that Dżok wasn't there and some tobacco leaves had been torn off. He walked around for a long time, calling and searching for Dżok – he thought that thieves must have poisoned him. After a fruitless search, he returned and we all sat down to eat like it was a funeral meal. Suddenly, we were delighted to see Dżok - tired and sad with a head injury and a bloody ear. He sat next to me, put his head on my lap and gave me a tormented look. Dżok recovered and helped us again, but what had happened that night remained his secret.

One day Nikołaj went to town and when he got back, he was quiet and pensive.

"Pola Don," he suddenly said in the evening, "a friend from the town has recommended a shepherd to me. I'm thinking about taking him in. It will mean more work for you, for you would need to feed him and pack him off to the fields. But he would help a little too – perhaps he'd also help with the pigs? With four of us adults, he'd have some food, too."

He wasn't asking my permission – he was simply thinking out loud.

The next morning, Nikołaj harnessed the horse, went off to town again and returned later with the shepherd.

"I've brought Jachimczik," he announced.

"God bless," said Jachimczik, a little bit too loudly, and took his too-big hat off in an exaggerated motion.

Everything he had was too big for him, from hat to shoes. He was ten or eleven years old and had an honest face with curious eyes.

"Jachimczik, you need to listen to Pola Don – she will feed you," advised Nikołaj and Jachimczik looked at me with a childish smile as if to say: "I'm not scared of her at all." And so from the first day, a thread of kindness or maybe even friendship entered into our relationship. At any rate, we got on very well.

It was clear that the boy had been starved from how ravenously he ate. So I made an effort to fatten him up. Besides what he had been wearing when he'd arrived, he had no spare clothes or underwear. Mom took some of Nikołaj Aleksandrowicz's unused clothes and altered them so they would fit him. Nikołaj was good to him. However, he was most attached to me

– after returning from the fields, he wouldn't leave my side, helping out with various jobs – feeding dogs and pigs, collecting vegetables from the garden.

Jachimczik slept on a pile of hay in the barn.

One evening, after a very hot day, I decided to also sleep on the hay. I made a bed not far from him and for a long time just lay down, unable to sleep. Jachimczik was snoring quietly next to me, sometimes anxiously changing position; at times his snoring was stopped by sniffling like he had a runny nose and at one point I heard violent weeping. I moved closer to him and tried to poke him awake , but he turned his back to me, and I was not sure whether he was trying to calm down or fall asleep. He didn't respond to my questions about whether he'd had a bad dream or perhaps someone had harmed him. Eventually we both fell asleep. The whole day images of the night kept reappearing in my mind. I felt sorry for the boy. I didn't know how to help him, especially since just like in the night, he didn't feel like talking to me during the day either. He looked sad and frowned at me with a mixture of embarrassment and fear.

In the evening, after work, Nikołaj and I went out to the tobacco field to plan for tomorrow and there I told him everything.

"Pola Don," said Nikołaj, "I'll tell you the truth. Jachimczik is a Jewish child. His father had a small food stall in town. Whenever I had difficulties, he always gave me credit. I repaid him whenever I could. He was a good man. When I went to town – that time when I came back and mentioned taking on a shepherd – people told me that his parents had been murdered. The Germans herded people into the barn and set it on fire. Jachimczik was walking with his parents to that barn, but some people pulled him out of the crowd and hid him among them. The Germans didn't notice. And he stood amongst the people and saw the barn on fire and heard the screams of people being burnt alive, his parents included. At first, he didn't eat at all. He cried for days on end. I approached him and he just sat looking blankly at me. I felt so sorry for him that it broke my heart. And then I asked: 'Jachimczik, would you come with me and be a shepherd?' And he said: 'I will go with you. Father said that you are a good person,' and he cried. I told him I would come back and get him – he looked at me doubtfully, like my leaving was taking the last of his hope away from him. After all I'd heard and seen, my mind wasn't in the right place, because at the end of the day I could have taken him straight away."

Jachimczik and I never talked about it. I admired his consistent commitment to playing the role of shepherd. Nobody could have guessed that a Dawidek or Chaimek from the Jewish town was hiding behind that boy.

After that night, his attitude towards me became even warmer, although at the same time it was marked with fear. Perhaps he was afraid that I had figured out his secret? Perhaps he was ashamed of crying, of his moment of weakness? Maybe I had become closer to him, and he was afraid of losing me? And perhaps he had guessed my own secret? In those times, a child's life age didn't necessarily match their calendar age. They grew up very fast. Jachimczik had suddenly matured on the day when he'd witnessed a mass murder in which he lost his parents. But still, despite this forced maturity, there was still evidently a childlike need for warmth, maybe affection, or simply the need of a mother. I could see a spark of joy, perhaps even happiness, when before going to the fields, he devoured his breakfast, vigorously chewing a slice of bread with cheese, washed it down with milk fresh from the cow and said, "God bless you" as I put my hand on his neck, kissed his forehead and said, "Go with God, Jachimczik."

Once I had to run an errand in Vilnius. I was absent for five days or more. When I came back, Mom shared that she had a huge problem with Jachimczik – he didn't want to eat at all.

"I'll eat when Pola returns," he said, when she tried to convince him.

Mr. Marianek sometimes visited us at Nikołaj's. Always with gifts from Kiezik – hulled grains, flour, lard. Ever since Jachimczik had moved in with us, Nikołaj was more and more often lost in thought, kind of anxious. Sometimes he drank but never excessively. Was he scared?

"Mr. Marian, how did it happen that we found our way here?" I asked him one day.

"Once, old Kiezik let me know I should come to his place, that he had some business here," he explained, "and I went. He told me about you and said: 'We need to arrange something for the engineer's wife and daughter. You know lots of people, try to find out where there's a good place.' I spent a day or two driving around the area, I checked here and there – tried to find out what was going on, if there were any strangers, which places had been examined by police or Germans. I eventually came to Nikołaj Aleksandrowicz. I've known him for a long time. He treated me to vodka and was always happy to talk to someone. One thing led to another, and I asked: 'Listen, Nikołaj, would you take on two female doctors from Vilnius?' He pouted and said: 'Why are you coming to me with this? There is an estate not far away and they have everything in abundance. People still come and go there, they stay, eat and drink. Two more women living with them would not make them any poorer.' So I responded: 'You know, it's really busy there and they are Jewish.' He contemplated my request and asked: 'Would you take them if you were me?' 'I think I would,' I said, 'it's remote here, not many people come around. It's not on the Germans' path or perhaps they are scared – woodlands are near. I think I would take them in.' Nikołaj thought for a while and said: 'If you would do it, then I won't be worse than you. Bring them.' So I brought you."

It was hard to believe this choice had had such a straightforward motivation. But it's true.

Father also came a few times. The first time was when I'd just managed to successfully bake my first ever loaf of bread. Obviously just seeing him caused our hearts to overflow with joy. After those initial emotions, we were able to talk about our life in Nikołaj's home. How proud he was of my achievements – baking, milking. How abundantly he showed it. In such a way that only he could.

Mom felt the same but showing emotions wasn't easy for her. In any case, they both realized that my attitude was the result of many years of them instilling in me this approach to work – a rule that whatever one does, one must try to one's best abilities, that it wasn't important what one did, but how one did it. It saved me a lot of unpleasant experiences. I met many people who would have seen the work I was doing as demeaning, meanwhile, thanks to my parents, I was able to take small satisfaction and joy from it.

After the war, we met the mother of my school friend – she was lost, had nowhere to go, nothing to eat. Mom took her in – at that time we were working and receiving some food from our patients in the villages. I remember when the poor thing was cooking a chicken we got from the village or frying scrambled eggs and talked to herself with compassion – 'is this really me? I can't even recognize myself.'

And she didn't have much to offer – she had simply been the pretty wife of a wealthy engineer, had no profession and no life ambitions. A poor "housewife" – as Mom and I would call her among ourselves.

We stayed at Nikołaj's until late summer of 1942, when out of the blue new complications arose. Nikołaj received a message that Mom needed to report to the Gestapo in town. He became understandably terribly anxious but tried to remain calm. He said that he would go with Mom and take a goose and some vodka with him.

They left in the morning. All day long I didn't know what to do with myself, I was a mess and couldn't eat anything. Jachimczik's eyes followed me fearfully, in silence.

Nikołaj only returned in the evening, a bit tipsy, and alone. Everything seemed tragically obvious.

"Where is my mom? Is she alive?"

"I don't know," he replied, avoiding my eye.

"How can you not know? You went together! What happened?"

"On our way, we decided that your mother would stay on the wagon, and I would go in to try and sort it out, so they would leave us alone; I would bribe them. And that's what happened. I waited at first, then I tried to explain our situation and asked them what they wanted from my cousin. I explained that she had no means to live in the city and had come to me, that she helps on the farm – I gave them vodka, a goose, drank with them and left without assurance, as they hadn't said anything. Your mother was not on the wagon. I walked around the street, asked people if they had seen where the woman who was sitting on my wagon had gone, I looked around in the neighboring streets. No one had seen anything. I was so scared to come back home. I have no idea where she has gone."

We did not know what to do next. Nikołaj suggested he harness the horse at dawn and go again to the town; perhaps he would find something out, although we had no hope that this would help in any way; in the end, he did not make the trip.

In the meantime, unexpectedly, Mr. Marian arrived. He had come to get me, and he told me that last night Mom had turned up exhausted at Kiezik's and begged him to come and get me as soon as possible.

We found out that, when Nikołaj Aleksandrowicz didn't come out for a long time, Mom had concluded that it was a bad sign and decided she had nothing to wait for. She got off the wagon and calmly walked away. Once she was out of the town, she asked peasants she encountered how to get to the village of Zahacie. She knew that she could find her way to Kiezik from there. She thought that the most urgent matter was to take me away from the area.

We were on our way within half an hour and in the evening I saw Mom and Father. When I saw them, I felt both joy and pain. How exhausted they were!

All was ready when I arrived. Dear Kiezik had planned and prepared everything.

Aloszka's Zameczek Settlement and the Niewiarowicz Family

Mom was transported to the Zameczek settlement, a few kilometeres from Zahacie, to Wincuś and Jadzia Aloszka. The next day, I was moved to Hipolit and Halina Niewiarowicz, on the outskirts of Zahacie. Father stayed at the mill, Rózia in her hiding place. She did not find out about our troubles until after they were over.

New people appeared on our way. We lived not far from each other and kept in touch. Father visited Rózia, came to see me, usually on Saturday nights, then we went to see Mom at Aloszkas', spent Sunday at their place and on Sunday night returned each to our own place.

It sounds idyllic, but it wasn't at all. Over the course of those few months of displacement, there was always something going on.

Soon after we were relocated to different places in the area, Mr. Nikołaj Aleksandrowicz Łapicki turned up – and asked about us in the villages. Kiezik was already aware that he was searching for us and decided that it was better for him not to know. When he reached the mill, Kiezik told him that we had been there but had left.

He thought that Nikołaj was a weak, timid man who often drank. Nikołaj asked him to pass a message on to us if possible, that he really liked us and wished us well. This story was very painful for Mom and myself. If you believed it to be true that he was a cowardly man, then you would view his attitude towards us and Jachimczik in a new light. How much more resilience, strong will and deep conviction would one need in order to overcome fear and weakness, to do what was right and to do what he did.

We were not afraid of Nikołaj, and at the very least would have gladly thanked him for everything. But conversation with Kiezik was short.

"Why would he need to know where you are? This is not the time."

Maybe he was right. After all, our contact with him could risk the lives of everyone dragged into the orbit of our curse. That was not an option.

And just like that, we never saw Nikołaj Aleksandrowicz again. We only found out bits of information about him after the war in Vilnius.

Years later, soon after the liberation of Vilnius on the 16th of July 1944, when we had jobs and a place to live, three young men around 20-22 years old came to us and asked if we knew Nikołaj Aleksandrowicz Łapicki.

"Yes, we do."

"Is it true that he hid you for some time?"

"Honest truth. Why do you ask?"

"During the war we were in those areas in a partisan army and often came over to Łapicki to get food. At first, he shared with us without a word, even gladly. But one time, he said that he had nothing to give. 'The Germans take it, you take it, how can I have enough?' – he said. We didn't believe him and like you do in the partisan army, we threatened him. 'Leave me alone. If I had it, I'd give it to you. I'm not serving the Germans. I've even had two Jewish female doctors from Vilnius living with me. They know the truth and would vouch for me. Their name was Komaj. But I don't know where they are now.' So we left him alone, but it always intrigued us whether he'd been telling the truth and when we found out about you, we decided to look into it."

They also told us that the Germans had shot Mr. Łapicki and burnt his house for helping the partisans. They didn't know anything about Agnieszka Josipowna or Jachimczik.

After some time, Mr. Marian arrived at Kiezik's house one night. He had orders to deliver Father to Stara Wilejka. He had come to warn us. They agreed that Father would disappear from the mill and Marian would come to get him in the morning. He would search for him, have an argument and then report at Stara Wilejka that "the engineer had run away, he's not at the mill." Father moved again to the ranger station. Everything was going as planned.

After a short time, Mr. Marian informed us that no one was pressing him to carry out the order, they'd probably forgotten about it. He thought that Father could look after the mill again. Everything kind of went back to the way it was before, but all of the people taking part in this game were uncertain and anxious.

Meanwhile, the Soviet partisans appeared in the areas surrounding Zameczek. Zameczek was a settlement containing five farms belonging to five cousins and a common banya[10]. They were hardworking, economical and agreeable people. All five families knew not only about Mom, but also about me and Father. They behaved like it was all normal. Mom helped Jadzia as much as she could on a daily basis, mainly looking after the boys, repairing underwear and tidying up the house. There was enough food. The hosts were kind and respectful towards her. Father and I visited Zameczek every week or fortnight. The only thing troubling Mom were fleas. I remember one of the conversations my parents had.

---

10   "banya" - sauna, originally a Russian steam bath with a wooden stove

"I can't stand it, the fleas will eat me," Mom said.

"Mareczka, you really astonish me," Father replied, "what kind of problem is that? You're staying with wonderful people, they are good to you, risk their lives for us. After all, you are the doctor, try to use that, teach them hygiene."

"I have no idea what to do with these fleas," Mom responded. "Jadzia's house is not dirty."

"You see?" Father said, "even you don't know how to deal with it, and you expect Jadzia to know. The fleas are not a disaster."

Indeed, Jadzia and Wincuś were incredible.

During our Sunday visits, in the morning, Jadzia first of all prepared a bath for us. There was a large barrel in the kitchen. Jadzia boiled water in a few big kettles and poured it in the barrel. Father always helped her. Next to the barrel, she put two buckets with cold and hot water for topping up, gave us a big metal mug, towel, and soap and the kitchen was turned into a bathroom. All three of us took turns bathing. It was like a ritual. The hosts took their bath in the banya.

After this amazing bath, our hair and bodies clean and washed, we would have a late Sunday breakfast.

Jadzia laid down a clean towel on a table, put down a plate with molten pork fat and lardons, another one with cream, sometimes some cheese, and between them and getting bigger by the second was a pile of blinis, twenty something centimeters wide, baked in the big oven on burning coals, on a big frying pan, which was put in and taken out with a long bar with a handle. I always admired the skill and speed with which she did it. Each of us took a hot blini by hand from the pile, rolled it up and dipped it in the cream or pork fat. What an amazing feast we had at that family table.

Not long after Mom arrived at Wincuś', the Soviet partisans appeared in the nearby forest. Zameczek was surrounded by vast woodlands and one could hear only the sounds of the wind and the ominous howling of wolves calling each other to gather in packs led by she-wolves. During that time, when we walked to Mom at night, we took bundles of straw and matches in case we ever encountered them – wolves are scared of fire.

There was talk that the whole forest was full of partisans. They would turn up in a few villages every night. They asked for and received or took away food, leaving "a receipt." They started to show up at the nearest settlement to them, Zameczek. The first house closest to the forest was Wincuś' house and I think that they had the closest contact with him. In the beginning, they came to eat but once they knew each other better, they would book the banya for the night. With time, they popped in during the day, usually on Sundays.

Wincuś introduced Mom as an auntie from the town who had no resources there to live on. They seemed to believe it. They called Mom "tiotiuszka" (an auntie). In fact, only the commander and his deputy came over. Both were intelligent. The commander, a tall, powerful man with blond hair, claimed that he was from Moscow, a historian or an art historian and introduced himself as Wiaczesław Wołostych. His deputy was much shorter, slender and brown-haired, and claimed to be an engineer from Kronstadt – Michaił Chołodienko. Whether there was any truth in their identities, it's hard to say.

For some time Wincuś tried to coordinate our visits so they wouldn't overlap with Wiaczesław and Michaił's. But he couldn't keep us separated for long. During one of those visits, while Wincuś was in the barn and Jadzia was preparing breakfast, Michaił sat next to Mom, who was sitting on a bench by the table, holding the little one.

"And you, Auntie, are you staying here 'on the bird's right'?" he asked unexpectedly.

Mom pretended that she didn't understand.

"What do you mean, 'on the bird's right'?"

"Are you hiding?"

"Yes," Mom confirmed, surprising herself.

"A Jew?"

"Yes."

"Don't worry, Auntie, we won't let you be harmed. Are you here alone?"

He was so endearing that Mom told him about all of us, who we were, where Father and I were staying. Michaił listened to Mom very carefully, was kind and patted her back warmly.

"Well," he said, "there will be a festival on our street too." (A Russian proverb.)

Some time passed and we all began to meet occasionally at Jadzia's Sunday breakfast. Warm relations formed.

Michaił and Father had their own technical topics to discuss. Wiaczesław and Mom competed in their knowledge of classic Russian literature.

At times, we were even privy to operational plans.

Once, Wiaczesław sent his unit to blow up a German train carrying ammunition. Michaił was eager to take part in the action. Wiaczesław was opposed to it, as he wanted to go alone. After a heated argument, Michaił got his way and Wiaczesław was the one who stayed behind. He spent the night enormously anxious, listening out for an explosion, checking his watch every few seconds and endlessly pacing the room back and forth. The operation was a success and everyone returned in one piece.

Sometimes, on their way back from their nightly adventures, as the partisans passed by "my headquarters," they would knock on the window, wake me up and take me to Mom. The first time, it was Mr Hipolit who was woken up.

"Who is it?"

"Partisans."

"What do you want?"

"Let Pola get dressed, we'll take her to her mother."

"Will you go?" asked Hipolit, anxious and uncertain whether it was the right thing to do.

"I will go," I replied.

Afterwards, I often took this journey to Mom with them, and Father would take a shortcut and come by himself.

At Kiezik's mill, following the uncompleted order of delivering Father to Stara Wilejka, everyone was on edge, and a sense of fear was growing. The thought of moving out of the area became more and more realistic. Lots of people knew about us. They were kind. We weren't scared of them, but we were aware it would take only one unkind person for our situation to change dramatically. This topic surfaced all the time in our conversations with Father.

Misza knew more and more about our situation and was concerned about our problems. He was very kind and genuinely wanted to help.

One day he announced that Father needed to leave the mill and that he would look around the area. He did as he said.

After one of the nightly operations, he came and announced that he'd found a place for Father.

"A house tucked away," he said, pleased with himself. "The people are trustworthy, it is a small farm, but well looked after, enough food. Father will have his own room. He can stay there and write."

Father had a technical book in French and in his "free time" he translated it, believing that one day it would be useful.

"I'll supply papers," Misza said, "and don't worry about Father. I warned them that if a hair of his head should perish, I'd burn the whole village down."

How they understood nothing!

"Misza," I said, "Father won't go there. The people here are good, generous, they have a deep sense of justice. Everybody struggles to make a living and we've been here for over a year staying for free in many different homes. They've shared with us everything they have and even though we've tried our best to be useful wherever we stayed, it's nothing compared to the risk they are taking. They might pay with their lives, even their whole families, for helping us. None of us will live with someone who feels threatened to take us in. No one here deserves that. What's more, a situation like the one you're describing doesn't guarantee our safety – under such circumstances anyone would get rid of a lodger forced upon them at the first opportunity."

"You forget that we are in the middle of a cruel war and this is no time for philosophizing," he said, trying to defend his idea.

He didn't understand and was disappointed that I wasn't appreciative of his good will. He seemed almost offended.

Nevertheless, my decision was final, and I didn't even talk to Father about it because I already knew he would share my opinion.

In the meantime, autumn arrived, and it was beginning to get colder. Once, on our way to Mom, Misza asked if I had warmer clothes for winter. I didn't.

After a short time, knowing that I was going to be at Mom's, he turned up, very pleased with himself – with a sheepskin coat, "a gift" for me.

"How did you get it?" I asked.

"I took it from a farmer. He had lots of things, and many sheepskin coats."

"Misza, I can't use it. Please take it back to its owner," I protested.

"You're being unreasonable. It's not a loss for them. They will stay in one place, while you might need to run away any minute. You may need to wander in the woodlands. You would freeze to death."

"Misza, I can't take the coat. Please, take it back."

"All right, I'll take it back. I hope you don't end up regretting this," he said, offended.

Even though he had good intentions, somehow his help wasn't well received by us.

Only as we were leaving the area and saying goodbye, was his last attempt successful. He simply handed me a fountain pen and a small bottle of ink.

"I hope you can take it as a keepsake," he said.

I didn't even ask anything, I accepted the gift and I used that pen for a long time after the war, until it got lost during one of our moves.

One night, Father came to me looking very anxious. News had reached the mill that the Germans were planning a partisan manhunt. He thought that we needed to warn them through Wincuś and take Mom out of Zameczek. We went to Zameczek that night. We quietly knocked on the door. Only Wincuś woke up and opened the door.

"What's happened?" he whispered.

"Nothing has happened yet, but something might. We need to be prepared," Father explained the situation. "The partisans need to be warned. For now, we'll take Mareczka with us until things become clearer."

"I will warn the partisans and prepare some weapons if needed. A girl who is staying at my cousin's needs to be moved somewhere else. She is also a Jew, from Świr. And where are you going to take Mareczka? Where is she going to walk on her swollen legs? Let her sleep and go away."

"We'll take her to the mill or to Pola's, then we'll see," Father replied.

"She won't go anywhere. If she were to die, it would be over my dead body. We all have weapons here. Don't worry. Go with God, otherwise you'll wake everyone up."

He didn't let us in the house.

Soon it turned out that the rumors were more than just gossip. The next night the Germans surrounded the forest. We could hear shooting. They didn't come to Zameczek. No one went to the forest, either. None of the partisans showed up in Zameczek. No one knew what played out that night in the forest.

Everyone sat quietly in their homes. No one from the village came. And no one from Zameczek went to the village.

A few days later, Wiaczesław and Michaił came at night – they were much changed, slimmer, exhausted. They told us about their experiences. Wincuś had managed to warn them about the danger, but the attack happened the next night after we'd visited his house. The Germans started by setting a fire all around the forest. Wiaczesław believed that they had no chance of fighting and ordered each person to try to escape the siege on their own. Those who survived were meant to report at a chosen place and time. After a few days, six of them gathered. One boy was missing – Kostia. That was how we found out with surprise that there were only seven of them. Just like everyone in the area, we were convinced that the forest was full of partisans. It was a result of their strategy. They showed up every night in many villages. When during the day, news about their operations spread, it turned out that they had been seen in many places. This multiplied their numbers in people's imagination. In reality, it was the same group of several people moving very quickly from one place to another.

But let me come back to the account of that night.

The partisans started a fruitless search for Kostia. Once they'd lost all hope of finding him, they came to Zameczek for help and advice. They wanted to know what had happened to him – whether he had died, been injured or was perhaps taken. If he'd died, they wanted to bury the body, if he was still alive – they wanted to help him. Wincuś suggested that his older boy, 11-year-old Janek, could go to the forest, "for mushrooms" – maybe he would stumble upon some trace of him. In the morning, they gave Janek a basket and sent him to search for any signs. In the evening, Janek returned with an empty basket, breathless and very nervous.

"I found Kostia, wounded, shot in the leg and so exhausted that I couldn't even sit him up."

After he was shot, Kostia had crawled out of the forest to a small, old cemetery nearby and lain down under a ledge protruding out from a tombstone. He'd covered himself with some leaves and lain down hungry and unable to move.

That night, they organized a rescue mission for Kostia. One of the Aloszeks harnessed a horse and together with two or three others, with Janek as their guide, went out to get Kostia. They brought him back to Zameczek, hid him in a barn belonging to one of Wincuś' cousins, fed him, and Mom put a temporary dressing on him. His leg was seriously injured – open with broken bones, Kostia was devastated.

Mom didn't have any medications, tools or dressings. She set the bones as best she could, made a cast by attaching the leg to a wooden plank and bandaged it using pieces of linen which had been boiled, dried in the sun and ironed, but a "window" was left where the wound was. Somebody found a bit of iodine. She changed the dressing through that window. Kostia's chances of healing were minimal. He was at grave risk of infection and suppuration – it wasn't certain when or even whether the bones would grow back together at all. However, his general condition improved day by day. Kostia's young body was fed well, nursed and surrounded by kindness, and he showed great resilience.

Not long after, the partisans decided to leave the area – they wanted to cross over the front line to the Soviet Union, to deliver Kostia to a hospital and then get back into the fighting, wherever they were directed.

One night they loaded Kostia onto the wagon of one of the Aloszkas; one person drove whilst the others walked alongside, armed. Kostia lay down on the wagon.

After a heartfelt farewell, the convoy went off and I never heard about their fortunes again. Did they get through the front line? Did any of them survive the war? Did Kostia endure this difficult journey? Did he keep his leg? All these questions remained unanswered.

In the meantime, at the home of Mr. Hipolit and Mrs. Halina Niewiaro-wicz, where I was staying, the food was dwindling. There were fewer potatoes and we ate them sparingly. Every time I ate a potato and saw the children – 11-12-year-old Zosia, EIa a few years younger, and little 4-5-year-old Hipek (Hipolit junior) – eating ravenously, I felt like I was choking on guilt.

Theirs was a very good family. Mr. Hipolit was the brother of Mr. Hieronim, the owner of a nearby estate; the same one who'd rescued us from Sobolewski's hands. It was common knowledge that Mr. Hieronim had been disinherited by his father due to his marrying a peasant woman. He'd tried his luck in America. The money he'd earned there was only enough to build a house, where they lived poorly, yet happily.

When I moved to their place after leaving Łapicki, the children were sick with trachoma. I nursed them. The disease was not advanced and my patients healed quickly.

Once I shared my doubts with Mr. Hipolit and asked if he could help me find a place to stay somewhere else.

"But why? The kids are healthy now, praise God for that," he replied. "You can teach them now."

I had it good with these people. I stayed gladly. The children became attached to me. The girls were eager to learn. Little Hipek usually sat on my lap, cuddled me and happily accompanied us. I had an especially close bond with Irka, who perhaps understood my situation, even though we tried not to talk about certain matters in the presence of the children. At that time, children matured quickly and often understood more than adults thought. And I genuinely liked them. That made my situation even harder.

"Mr. Hipolit, there is not much food left over, it's so difficult for you. I'm constantly thinking that I'm eating the children's portions. Should I try to move somewhere? Maybe you know of other opportunities?"

"Miss Pola, what are you talking about? We've eaten together the entire winter, we'll be hungry together in spring," he replied.

I stayed again.

However, the Germans who were furious about their unsuccessful operation gave the locals a hard time.

Our presence in the area became more and more dangerous both for us and for those who'd taken us in, even though they didn't say a word to us. We became increasingly convinced that we should do something about it.

Looking for New Opportunities

We had exhausted every possibility in the area. We needed new contacts to move somewhere else. One of us had to go looking for new opportunities. It could only be me. Father, as a man, was already in a riskier position. Różka, for obvious reasons, could not even be considered. Mom had the right "look" and way about her, however, she had changed, and her resilience was not what it had been. In normal times, she was energetic, joyful and full of initiative, but now she was severely depressed and couldn't cope in such circumstances. What's more, her health was failing – the swelling in her leg had increased. To make matters worse, we were without Aryan papers and had no proof of identity to evidence our innocence and show we were on the "Aryan" side.

Mom barely took any part in our discussions about it. She said that she would do whatever "the team" decided. My father and I were "the team." We decided that I would go to Vilnius and try to get hold of papers, come up with new contacts and look for opportunities to move. Father advised me to stay, if possible, at Stanisław Frąckiewicz's, our first place of refuge. If that proved impossible, I was meant to look for other possibilities among the contacts he suggested: Władysław Frąckiewicz, priest Jankowski, doctor Hurynowicz, engineer Obrompalski, our housekeeper Emilia. Even if I didn't stay at Stanisław Frąckiewicz's, he instructed me to leave a message there about my whereabouts in case they needed to find me.

I took with me our professional certificates, most importantly the graduation diplomas and work references. Keeping them safe and in good condition became increasingly difficult. When we'd removed them from their last hideout, a metal box buried under the hard earth floor of a barn, they were covered in damp patches. After drying them in the sun, they were partially crumbling. I was instructed to leave them somewhere safe in Vilnius.

It was already January 1942. A beautiful, sunny, snowy winter. Around December 10th, I left by sledge for Vilnius with a peasant whom I did not know. The previous evening, I said goodbye to Mom. I asked Father to pass my love to Różka, whom I hadn't seen for some time and in the early morning I said goodbye to Father as well on a snowy forest road bathed in sunshine. We stood hugging each other in silence for a long time – our embrace did the talking for us. I could barely stop my tears. Eventually Father let me go from his arms and looked at me sadly.

"Well, go on my dear," he said. "Be brave and careful. I will send the sledge for you in ten days' time."

I sat on the sledge, wrapped myself up in a hooded greatcoat and prepared to embark into the unknown.

"Farewell, Daddy," I struggled to say, a lump in my throat.

"Don't say farewell, say, see you soon."

"See you soon," I tried again.

Though it would be our final farewell.

I looked very different. The potato diet had added a lot of kilograms. I was dressed like a peasant – in Różka's sheepskin coat and a large, grey, woollen shawl which covered my head. It crossed over at the front and was tied up at the back in a big knot which served as a bag; I also had a basket and felts. This fortunately became a good disguise. Even my friends would struggle to recognize me.

The journey was quiet. Mr. Frąckiewicz received me kindly and let me stay at his place. I began my search for contacts the next morning.

In the early morning, I paid my first visit to engineer Obrompalski. I had been absent from city life for some time and I arrived at his door a few minutes after seven, when in the city, people would usually still be asleep. A servant opened the door. She looked sleepy and begrudgingly glanced at my basket as if she were expecting a delivery.

"What do you want?" she asked reluctantly.

"I would like to see engineer Obrompalski," I informed her.

"He is still sleeping. What business do you have with him?"

"I need to speak to him myself."

The engineer, awoken by our conversation, peeked out from behind the door.

"Have you come to see me, miss?" he was surprised.

"Yes," I smiled, hoping he would recognize me. But he didn't.

"What is it?"

The servant, intrigued by the whole situation and not used to women having business with her employer, certainly at this time of day, didn't move.

"Do you not recognize me, sir?" I whispered. "I am Pola."

He had known me since I was twelve years old and remembered me as a slender, pretty, well-dressed student.

"My child, I didn't recognize you at all. Come in, take off your coat. "Make us some breakfast," he said to the shocked servant and showed me into the house.

I could hear the nervous hustle of an unhappy servant in the kitchen; she was banging pots as though in an effort to express her resentment towards the engineer receiving this strange woman and making her serve her. It made me uncomfortable and the engineer noticed it.

"Don't worry," he said. "You're in no danger."

As we ate breakfast, I told him our story and explained our current situation and needs. He had no solutions on the spot, but promised to look around, think it over and asked me to return in a few days.

In the evening, I went to priest Jankowski. He lived in the same place at the vicarage next to the All-Saints church. The church bordered with the ghetto. An old housekeeper opened the door.

"Please come in, sit down. The priest is having a nap but it's time to get him up anyway."

She led me into a room and pointed to an armchair. The room was small, furnished with a large table and chairs, a dresser and some holy pictures. The cross. Silence. Darkness.

Not long after, the priest appeared – an old, slim man with incredibly kind eyes.

"God bless you," he greeted me. "What has brought you here?"

I introduced myself as the daughter of engineer Komaj, whom the priest had offered to help at the beginning of the war.

"I know, I know, my child. I remember. Tell me, how are your father and mother? How are you managing?"

I had to tell the story and explain our situation and needs again. He gave me supper. He listened to me carefully and said that he would try to acquire birth certificates for me and Mom. He thought that Father would do better with an *Ausweis*[11].

"I can't sort it out by myself, but I will contact another priest, maybe he will have an idea."

As I walked down the squeaking, wooden stairs, he guided my way with a kerosene light held in his left hand, all the while making the sign of the cross with his right hand.

"Go with God, child," he said as a goodbye.

When I returned a few days later, he gave me an original birth certificate from the Podbrodzie parish for the name of Zofia Januszkiewiczówna. Her age was similar to mine. He didn't have a certificate for Mom – he couldn't find one with a similar age and first name. He thought it was important for her to keep her real name.

"It's different for you," he explained. "You can get used to a new name, but your mother might find it difficult and betray herself if she does not respond to her new name."

He also gave me details of another priest who he said I could talk to about a document for Father. On a certain day and time I was supposed to go to the Saint Anna Church (a jewel of the Gothic style) and stand during the

---

11   "ID card" (German)

mass on the right-hand side of the nave with a newspaper under my arm. The priest would approach me immediately after the service. Indeed, that's what happened after the mass. He was tall, overweight, with a fat face and small, shifty eyes.

"Come tomorrow before seven o'clock in the morning to the Bernardines," he said quietly. "The gate will be locked. You'll need to ring. The janitor will know, he will bring you to me."

In the morning, I rang, and the gate opened.

"Follow me," said the janitor, and added nothing further.

He led me down a narrow sidewalk on the left-hand side of the courtyard to the staircase in the corner, then we walked through a corridor and up the stairs for what seemed to me a very long time. I lost my sense of direction. My heart was racing in my chest. There was something very strange, mysterious and even incredible in the silence that surrounded us. The quiet janitor, intricate passages and narrow, spiral staircase made me feel very uneasy. Although I tried to tell myself there was no reasonable basis for my anxiety, the atmosphere frightened me. Finally, we reached our destination. The door was opened by a priest in pyjamas. He apologized for his attire. He invited me into an office, situated at the end of a small hall. The room was bright, medium-sized but with two big windows. Most of the room was occupied by a massive desk and two large, soft, deep armchairs. From the office, a door-shaped opening without doors but with a curtain instead led to the next room.

Instead of excusing himself to go and get dressed, the priest began to explain that his morning routine took him a long time due to the lack of running water and that he had to use a shower device that he had made himself; he then pulled open the curtain and offered to show it to me.

I stood in the doorway. There was a large watering can attached to the ceiling with a rope, underneath it was a large basin and two buckets of water sat beside it. Even though it seemed obvious how the contraption worked, he took time to explain his shower system in detail. The room had no window, only a small opening in the ceiling above a huge wooden bed full of tousled bed linens. I listened to his comprehensive explanation, agreed that it was indeed problematic and retreated to the office, sitting down in the armchair. I offered to wait while he finished with his morning routine. But, unexpectedly, the priest declined my offer.

"Let's get straight to it," he said, sitting down behind the desk. "Generally speaking, I know what's going on, but I would like to know your father's age, his height and other characteristics. And I will need a photograph. Would you like some tea?" he offered.

I declined, lying that I'd already had breakfast and that I was in a hurry, because I had a lot of errands to run that day. He set another day for me to visit at the same time. But I never returned. I didn't trust him, his strange behavior made me feel, perhaps unjustly, scared.

Thankfully, I didn't see priest Jankowski again, so I didn't have to tell him about the contact he had given me or explain why it hadn't worked out.

I ended up acquiring a birth certificate for Mom totally by accident. I can't remember why I met Janka Jantzenówna, my friend from university who was one year younger than me. I'd visited her several times before the war. I remembered where she lived, and I suppose I just went to her house. Her father was a professor at Stefan Batory University. She was in a relationship with my school friend, doctor Szymon Remigolski, whom she later married.

"Wait a minute," she said, after listening to my story, "I think I've got a birth certificate belonging to my deceased auntie somewhere in a drawer, perhaps that'll work?"

It was a Russian birth certificate from the tsarist period with my Mom's year of birth and the name Maria Paszkiewicz on it. It fit like a glove. The certificate even met priest Jankowski's requirements – Mom's name was also Maria.

As I was writing this memoir, I contacted Janka and asked her for a photograph. We reminisced about old times. By the way, I found out that she never had an auntie with this surname. The birth certificate had been prepared for Szymon's mother, who unfortunately never got a chance to use it. Janka had told me this innocent little lie because she wanted to avoid a conversation about the source of the certificate and the potential risk involved in me knowing its true purpose.

My spirits were lifted. I did not know much about documents and to what extent they could help us. I wasn't aware that birth certificates were very valuable, especially when accompanied by an ID card or employment references. I thought that, apart from Father's documents, our issue was basically sorted out. I decided to visit a fellow university student whom I had befriended during a surgical residency in Warsaw. Her sister was an established dentist in Vilnius and had a telephone so I had no problem getting an address for my friend, Dr. Ksienia Lutomska. She was a dentist. She rented a room where she lived as well as received patients, and she used her landlord's living room as a waiting room during her working hours. The room was small, divided in half by a wardrobe with a sofa behind it. In the first half, opposite the window, were a dentist's chair and professional equipment. Behind the wardrobe were the sofa and a dresser. Both parts were kind of joined together by a small table and three chairs. Ksienia received me so kindly that for a moment I forgot that there was a war going on, that I was illegal, that I was a kind of 'untermensch'.[12]

I visited her while she was working. She left me to settle on the sofa behind the wardrobe while she received patients. After she finished, she made us tea, brought some cake, and we talked at the table about our experiences. I confided in her about our current problems. I found out that she had a few German patients.

"I think that one of them is a good person," she said. "He helped me send a parcel to my nephew in Stutthof; not for free but it doesn't matter. Should I talk to him about issuing a document for your father?" she suggested. It felt natural to agree. I arranged to come back in a few days' time, also during her working hours.

My next visit was similar to the first one. The German had brought Ksienia a document for Father. One of our friends had kept Father's new suit, and I used it to pay for the document. As we were agreeing on a date to deliver

---

12   underman, subhuman (German) – a Nazi term for non-Aryan, "inferior people"

the suit, someone knocked on the door and an acquaintance, another from our year at university, entered. He was well-known at the Stefan Batory University, an extremist National Democratic party activist, who for seven years of studies never contaminated himself by greeting, let alone shaking hands with, a Jew. The situation, to say the least, was awkward. I decided to go as quickly as possible to avoid leaving the place together with him. I stayed only for a bit, trying to keep up with the conversation, then I said goodbye.

"You know," Ksienia said at our next meeting, "after you left last time, K. asked me to tell you that you shouldn't be scared of meeting him at my place or on the street. He said, 'We do not collaborate with Germans or betray Jews to them. We'll sort them out ourselves after the war.'"

I didn't meet him again until 1948 when he was an assistant at a very famous clinic where I brought my husband for a diagnosis. "We haven't met," he said, is if we'd never known each other during all those years of studying.

I still had a few extra days until Father had promised to send the sledge for me. Happy with my "achievements," I tried to sort out our professional diplomas and also arranged a few additional meetings. After arranging a meeting over the phone, I met with Mr. Władysław Frąckiewicz somewhere on the street. He was very kind, asked me about everything and everyone and showed a full understanding about the importance of our documents.

"We'll do something about it," he said, after considering it for a moment, "but maybe in a day or two. My women," (he had a wife and two daughters) "are going away tomorrow and I'll think of something then. They don't need to know. No point in worrying them."

Once they'd gone, he invited me to his place. He had an idea. The kitchen stove didn't quite touch one of the walls, but left a gap of approximately 20 centimeters behind it. He chiselled out a hole in the wall and after drying the documents out a little, bricked over them.

"I'll paint the kitchen tomorrow. It'll be a surprise for their return. My wife will be happy, and the documents will be safe."

He fed me, let me stay overnight, and then we said goodbye. The next time I saw him was after the war when I came back to retrieve my documents.

I also made contact with my close school friend and university professor Chaim Hilel Fryd. He was in the ghetto with his mother. His father had already been taken away by the Gestapo and was murdered in Ponary.

I visited Ponary in 1975 during my stay in Vilnius – a place of mass executions, just outside Vilnius. Right next to the ditches dug up by Jews for their own deaths, now covered by green grass, in a little wooden house there was a small memorial chamber. In it were some photographs of people who had been murdered, including rabbi Fryd, Hilel's father, and professor Pelczar from the Stefan Batory University, our lecturer on general pathology.

An area called Kailis on Rydz-Śmigły Street was just beyond the main ghetto. Here, they gathered Jews who claimed to be furriers. Their job was to make sheepskin coats for the Nazi army for winter.

Fryd was a doctor at this Kailis, even though he still lived in the main ghetto. He had a pass allowing him to move between the ghetto and the Kailis. He used it to meet with me at the ruins of a house on Wingry Street. We told each other our life stories, I boasted about my recent achievements and showed him the acquired documents. When he saw Father's Ausweis, he was worried.

"This German tricked you. You can see straight away that it's a fake. I'm afraid that this document will carry more risk than benefit for you even just carrying it around, and certainly if your father were to use it."

I could see that it wasn't easy for him to say what he'd said. His short-sighted eyes were full of warmth and compassion. My euphoria was quashed. We went our separate ways, quite depressed.

I also made contact with Rózia's friend, who lived on the outskirts of the city, and our former housekeeper Emilia, who lived close to the ghetto on Mała Stefańska Street.

Rózia's friend offered me a place to stay for a few days if I needed it.

Emilia gave me a royal welcome. She lived in a small, dark flat that had probably previously belonged to Jews, in a house with a yard and a well, where like in a small town, people were always curiously peeking through their windows at any stranger, wondering from where and why she or he had come. This alone was shocking to me. What's more, Emilia, who had never been very emotionally stable, reacted incredibly loudly when she saw me.

"My dear miss, it's so good that you came!" she was heard by everyone. Her kindness moved me. She boiled a pot of water, almost washed me herself despite my protests, put me to bed, and gave me some milk.

She was very excited, fussed over me, asked me about everything and told me her own story.

Emilia was a very religious and devout woman. While she lived with us, she went to church every day before her morning errand of shopping for breakfast rolls. Once she didn't return for a long time and Mom went to look for her. She found her lying prostrated on the stone floor of an empty church. This happened from time to time.

Emilia was still in contact with one of my school friends, Masza Bialer, who lived in our pre-war apartment, in my room.

Emilia told me about life in the city and what she knew about life in the ghetto. She absolutely refused to agree to me leaving her before curfew. So, I stayed overnight. In the morning I heard movement outside and some barely audible shreds of conversations. Emilia quickly drew the net curtains so I could look out onto the street whilst remaining invisible from outside.

The Jews from the ghetto were being led to work. They filled the narrow street to the brim, dragging their feet on the cobblestones. Their greyish-yellow faces looked hopeless. They were emaciated to the limit, hunched. Sometimes they looked at the windows they were passing. Sometimes they whispered words to each other. I recognized a few friends among them. I was shocked. Emilia tried to pull me away from the window, but I couldn't stop looking at them. Feverishly, I looked for loved ones, friends, colleagues, even though it didn't matter. I couldn't help any of them in any way. I was tormented by the thought that maybe I should have been there with them, too.

"Miss, this is of no use. I see it every day and I still can't get used to it," Emilia tried to comfort me.

As I was saying goodbye, to my surprise, Emilia forced a coin into my hand – it was a golden 5-ruble coin.

I never saw Emilia again. I still have my family photographs.

The Disaster

I didn't really have anything else to sort out in Vilnius and began anticipating Father's sledge. I was still living with Mr. Stanisław Frąckiewicz, and I didn't leave the house to avoid unnecessary danger to my hosts and myself. The empty days were filled with anxiety. I had no doubt that Father would sort everything out, but at the same time the lack of news and sight of a sledge was weakening me mentally and the sinking feeling in my stomach grew. I was increasingly afraid for Father. Had something bad happened? With each passing day and hour the thought became progressively more intrusive until it filled my mind completely. I completely lost my appetite during those few days, I couldn't even stomach a bite. I was so overwhelmed with anxiety that I would spend hours pacing kilometers from one corner of the small room to the other. When I was around other people, I was unable to join in their conversations. My mood began to gradually impact the others. I was aware that I was making things worse but I just wasn't able to control myself.

One night, my host woke me up. I sat up straight on the bed.

"Are they here?!" I shouted.

"No, no one is here. Please calm down, miss," he thought I was asking about the Germans.

"Then what's wrong?" I asked.

"I woke you up because you were screaming terribly. You could hear it all through the house. I was afraid someone outside would hear it."

"Really?" I said, abashed. "I'm sorry."

Reassured, he left the room. My face and pillow were soaked with my tears. The incident had been triggered by a dream that still hovered before my eyes even after waking. It felt so real, like I was experiencing it for the second time.

I had dreamed that Father and I were walking to Mom like we used to do. But not through a field or forest road but through a swamp, in which our legs were sinking. The wet surface made a squelching sound each time we pulled our legs out. Father was in front of me, looking for firmer ground. The swamp became deeper and deeper. At some point, Father couldn't take his legs out of the mud and started to sink. I could see him becoming immersed in the muck, his eyes pleading with mine. 'Polunia, don't come here, don't come here!' he kept warning me. Terrified, I obeyed but asked, 'what can I do? Maybe tear off my clothes, throw them to you and pull you out?' Father responded: 'You can't help me, my dear. It has to be this way. Just don't come to me, go back, I beg you.' I could see Father sinking deeper and deeper before my eyes. I saw the swamp reaching his lips, his nose. I wanted to scream but I couldn't. Only once the mud had covered his mouth and Father had stopped talking to me did I begin to scream terribly. That was when someone grabbed my arm. It was my host.

I'm not much of a believer in mysticism and I don't consider this dream to be prophetic. It was simply my unconscious mind projecting my fears and anxieties.

It was hard to gather my thoughts: I was just helplessly waiting. I was making my hosts restless, and now, I was even interrupting their sleep. Was I going crazy? But what could I do?

I decided to move for a few days to Rózia's friend. This would give the Frąckiewicz family a break from me, setting them free from the questionable pleasure of hosting me. A change of scenery might also encourage me to pull myself together. I left my new address just in case the sledge arrived. Wincuś Aloszka found me there a few days later. However, he wasn't coming to get me. Instead, he had brought Mom and Rózia. He told me that Father had been taken by the Germans to Stara Wilejka and that together with Kiezik he'd decided to get them out of the area – Wincuś had come with them and Kiezik had gone to try to get Father released.

My initial instincts told me to go with Wincuś to the countryside. But it was hard knowing that it would take a miracle to free my father from the occupants' hands. On the other hand, if we stayed here we'd have to make arrangements for a place to stay. Three of us staying with my friends who had only agreed to take me in for a few days was out of the question. I also realized that I personally could not have come up with any better plan than Kiezik's. I had no doubt that he would do whatever it would take. I had to grit my teeth and do what I needed to do, here.

I cried all night, then got dressed early in the morning to go to the Frąck-iewiczes and tell them what had happened so they would not worry about me. As I was leaving, Wincuś stopped me in a hallway and held me by the arms.

"Pola," he said, "you need to be strong. Our Don is gone. You are the main head of the house now. I had to bring Mareczka and Rózia. Right now, it's dangerous for you there. Once things settle down, I will bring you back to the countryside to stay with us. But at the moment, everyone is talking. It's dangerous. If you have nothing to eat, let me know – I can always bring potatoes."

He was holding me in his arms and his heavy tears were dripping onto my head.

"It has to be this way for now," he said.

He left in the evening, leaving us some flour, hulled grains, lard and four sausages as big as pretzels sent from Hipolit's children. Each sausage had a card with a name tied to it and Irka, the eldest, had written: "It's better if that I do not see you, in case you do not live." Mr. Hipolit sent his assurance that we could always hide at his place if needed.

Wincuś was also the one who informed me later about Father's death. It was a Sunday. The forest ranger had gone to church with his wife and Father was alone in their house. That day, people saw Sobolewski sniffing around in the area. When the forest ranger and his wife returned home, the kitchen door was wide open. Father wasn't there. There were also no traces of any-body's presence in the house, and nothing was missing. They were alarmed and decided to go to Kiezik to inquire about Father. However, the mystery was solved before they got there – they stumbled upon Father's dead body. Someone later told them that he had been walking nearby when he saw Father running and Sobolewski pursuing him, shooting at him. One bullet hit. He saw Sobolewski approach the body but at that point the bystander got scared and slipped away.

Father's gold teeth crowns were missing, as well as his shoes, the old ones given to him by Jews in Pastavy; his jacket was undone and it looked like his pockets had been searched. The crowns and shoes were the only spoils of the murder. They suspected that Father had seen Sobolewski through the window (remembering him well after that memorable night), couldn't bear the tension, began to run away and that was his end. He died on the 31st of January, 1943.

After the liberation of Vilnius, I felt compelled to visit the Świr area where we'd experienced so much goodness and where we'd lost so much. I was desperate to see Kiezik. I had no material things I could give him in return for his help, and besides, was it even possible to repay him? I just wanted to hug him, kiss him – maybe say a few good words if I found anything appropriate to say.

I won't lie, I also wanted to know what had happened to Sobolewski. I had no specific intentions towards him. I don't know, maybe I wanted to hand him over to a justice system? Maybe I wanted to force him to look into my eyes? Perhaps I would find a way to show him such hate and contempt that he would remember for the rest of his life and understand just how much pain he'd caused us.

But Sobolewski wasn't there – he must have believed in Mr. Niewiarowicz's prophetic words that there would not be a place for him there anymore and run away with the Germans.

Kiezik was extremely pleased to see me. I felt like I was visiting a dear grandfather. He was so affectionate. However, we avoided talking about Father. It was too painful to open the unhealed wound.

Later that evening, the eldest daughter of Halina and Hipolit Niewiaro-wicz came over. We spent the night on hay.

In the morning after breakfast, Kiezik summoned up the courage to say to me:

"Well, let's go, I'll take you to the engineer's grave."

We walked along a forest road for some time in silence. I felt that he was very tense; he finally put his hand on my shoulder.

"You know," he said, "it happened this way: I buried the engineer in the forest and when I came back the next day – the grave had been dug up. I buried him again. But when they dug it up a second time, I buried him again and put up a cross. Then they left it alone. So I thought: if you survived, maybe you would come here and then do whatever you wanted with it. It's up to you, leave the cross or take it away."

We'd just reached a mound with a wooden cross. Father's ashes rested here.

"Let the cross stay, Kiezik. Thank you," I choked up and cried in his embrace.

I felt that he was happy with my decision. And Kiezik said, like he was trying to make sense of it, "I think it's good, because even though the engineer was not baptized, he had a Christian soul."

After I received the message of my father's death, my head was filled with the two sentences Wincuś had told me: "You are the head of the house now. It has to be this way." But how?

Rózia's friend was very composed, she barely addressed our presence, nor did she imply anything. This made me feel responsible. I set off to the city – with no plan, idea or strategy.

I'm of No Use to Anyone.

I can't remember how it happened, but at that time in Vilnius I crossed paths with Aleksander Smilg – a chemist whom I barely knew from before the war, a friend of one of my colleagues at university.

I told him about my situation. He offered to take me to a lady who would help me.

"But I have no means," I warned him.

"It doesn't matter," he replied.

He took me to see Maria Fedecka. She lived in a villa on Nowogródzka Street. There were some people in the house. The house seemed at peace, unaffected by the affairs raging beyond the fence. Muszka was charming, a little absent-minded, a bit too distracted and agitated for the hostess of a reputable home. She already knew my situation from Aleksander.

"I think that I will be able to place your mother in a safe place," she said after a short conversation.

She told me I would get confirmation in a few days. When I reported to her again, she was in a good mood.

"The matter is decided," she said without preamble. "In a day or two, your mother can go to a Lithuanian town to act as a nanny for a child of a young couple of doctors from Vilnius."

My reaction to the news surprised me. I didn't show any joy, I was completely numb.

"Are you not going to ask where your mother will be? Who these people are? Are you opposed to your mother leaving?" Muszka was surprised.

I wasn't happy, nor scared for Mom. It seemed like all of this was simply happening outside of myself. I felt nothing, I was empty inside, dead.

"Thank you very much," I managed to blurt out. "I fully trust you and I don't feel like I've got the right to ask for anything."

Only then did Muszka seem to notice my condition.

"You know this doctor," she said calmly, "you were in the same year of medical school. It's Wojtek Pogorzelski, and his wife is your younger friend from university and my sister. You will get news of your mother through her."

"Thank you. I can't imagine anything better."

The very next day, Mom left with Mima (Emilia Pogorzelska) to Sirvintos and as soon as they got there, she became Maria Paszkiewiczówna, as decreed on the birth certificate from Janka Jantzenówna's "auntie."

These are fragments of the reports from Dr. Emilia Pogorzelska and her doctor husband Wojciech Pogorzelski for the Jewish Historical Institute in Warsaw:

In autumn 1941, we moved to Sirvintos, a Lithuanian town, 50 kms from Vilnius, because my husband was granted permission to practice as a doctor by the Lithuanian government. On March 29th, 1942 our daughter Zosia was born. Both my husband and I collaborated secretly with the Home Army (AK) during the whole occupation. Lots of Poles lived in Sirvintos and the surrounding areas and the AK, well-organized by the local locksmith Franciszek Burdynowski, was active there.

As an AK courier, I often went to Vilnius. I was in close contact with Maria Fedecka (Muszka), my sister who was much older than me, who helped many Jews, some of whom she didn't even know at all. Her closest friends jokingly called her "Saint Jewish."

In winter 1942, my sister told me that she had no place for a female Jewish doctor, Mrs. Maria Komaj, whose husband, an engineer, had recently been murdered. She was in a bad state mentally, she was close to giving up and planned to go to the ghetto. My sister wanted me to take Mrs. Komaj with us to Sirvintos. I had no doubt that my husband and his family (his mother and brother lived with us) would approve of this decision which I made without consulting them.

The next day, together with Mrs. Maria, we hitchhiked to Sirvintos, which was the usual way we would travel there.

Mrs. Komaj, as I anticipated, was kindly received by my mother-in-law and brother-in -law, and my husband was glad to discover she was the mother of Pola Komaj, his university friend. Once we arrived, we agreed together on some of the details of her new identity. Because she spoke fluent French, we decided that she had been educated in a convent school in France (in fact, she actually had studied in France) and that she was my relative.

Mrs. Komaj's official duties were to look after my 8-month-old daughter Zosia. She was an amazing nanny, she had an incredibly kind and warm attitude towards our child and the child was drawn to her.

In the meantime, our new maid, whom I'd brought from Vilnius before Mrs. Komaj's arrival, started to suspect something and one day approached me, saying: "Zosia's nanny is Jewish and could harm your baby!"

I began to swear, crossed myself and vowed that Mrs. Maria was a Christian, that she'd gone to a convent school in France and that she was my relative. But unfortunately, the gossip that our nanny was a Jew began to circulate around the town and came back to our ears.

Once we even sent Mrs. Komaj together with my mother-in-law to church, however she felt morally conflicted and did not want to go again. So I decided to provoke the maid into an argument, and then I let her go and sent her back to Vilnius. Our maid seemed to believe me, but I couldn't know for sure if this was the case, so the best temporary solution for this difficult situation was for us to separate from her. And yet, the rumors didn't stop and soon my husband approached Franciszek Burdynowski (I already mentioned him – an organizer of the AK district Wiłkomierz), asking him to curb the circulating gossip, assuring him that Mrs. Komaj had an authentic birth certificate (and baptism certificate). Mr. Burdynowski promised to deal with it. We still have no idea how he did it, but the rumors ceased.

Mrs. Komaj stayed with us until July 1944. As the Soviet Army advanced, she went back to Vilnius to reunite with her daughter. During her time with us, she received some messages from her daughter, usually through me, because I made contact with Pola from time to time. Our 5-year-old daughter Zosia went to her "nanny" again in 1948 when I stayed in hospital to give birth to my second child. Afterwards, both Komaj ladies moved to Warsaw.

We stayed in touch by correspondence and occasionally in person. I visited Mrs. Komaj twice in Warsaw when she was ill. She died in 1972, and together with her family and friends we took her to her final resting place. She was a wonderful doctor and an amazing person. Good and brave. For all her post-war years, she worked in her speciality. She was a doctor with a calling and gave her whole heart to the sick.

When I took Mrs. Komaj to my house, I didn't think about the motives of my actions. I only knew that I had to do something for her, and this was a testimony to my protest against the enormous barbarism and cruelty – I needed this protest myself.

Dr. Emilia Pogorzelska

Doctor/docent Wojciech Pogorzelski's report:

From autumn 1941 until 1944 I was in Lithuania in the town of Sirvintos where I practiced as a doctor. My family living with me consisted of my wife, young daughter Zosia, mother and brother.

I came to Sirvintos right after the Nazis murdered all of the local Jews.

Despite my limited medical experience and young age, local people sought my help in large numbers.

In autumn 1942, my wife brought from Vilnius a female gynecologist, Maria Komaj, a Jew.

At the time, doctor Komaj was emotionally devastated by the recent news of her husband engineer Komaj's death. I believed it was my human responsibility *to provide her with protection and care. We employed her as a nanny for our 8-month-old daughter. After some time Mrs. Komaj overcame her deep depression. We quickly realized she was an amazing human being. Not only was she a perfect nanny for our daughter but she also had a just character and was an excellent women's doctor. Obviously, we had to hide not only her background but also her profession.*

Even so, she often helped with gynecological examinations, presenting herself as my "nurse," and then outside my office she would instruct me on symptoms, diagnoses and treatment. She also conducted surgeries with my assistance. During those surgeries, we convinced patients that I was the one operating and Mrs. Maria was simply assisting me by handing me surgical equipment.

My professional practice prospered and was especially popular among female patients.

Apart from my family, the truth about Mrs. Komaj was known only to locksmith Franciszek Burdynowski who is no longer alive. He was a permanent resident of Sirvintos, an AK solider (Home Army) and the Polish superior in this part of Lithuania. Once he managed to successfully quash rumors that Mrs. Maria was Jewish. At some point these rumors about her were spreading in Sirvintos.

Mrs. Komaj was respected in our home and treated like a member of the family. We parted after the Red Army arrived. Our friendship continued for years.

Doctor Komaj passed away in 1972 in Warsaw. She left behind her daughter, Pola Wawer, an ophthalmologist, with whom we also kept friendly contact.

Doctor/Docent Wojciech Pogorzelski

Naturally, later on Mom told me a lot about her stay in Sirvintos – indeed she felt like a family member and WAS grateful not just for it being a "refuge" but also because she liked the family and felt attached to them. Zosia, her ward, had a special place in her stories. She was a very pretty little girl with a stubborn and feisty character. However, Mom, with her consistent approach, gained authority over her and their relationship was not only proper but also warm. Mom loved Zosia very much.

After the repatriation, we ended up in Bielsko in Silesia while the Pogorzelskis were in Łódź. Mom dreamed about seeing Zosia. She missed her greatly. We were all busy with work and routine.

They final reunited in 1948 when the Pogorzelskis brought Zosia and left her with us in Bielsko for some time. Mom couldn't contain her joy. Zosia was still very beautiful and funny.

At that time, I was the manager of the Jewish Children's Home in Bielsko. When all three of us entered the Children's Home, a group of children surrounded Mom and one by one shared some problems they were having. Zosia observed the scene and listened, and afterwards she pulled me aside and asked:

"Pola, why do the children call Nanny 'a doctor'?" she whispered in my ear.

"Because your nanny is also a doctor and treats those children," I explained.

For a while she tried to make sense of my answer in her head.

"No, my mom is a doctor and treats children, not my nanny," she announced flatly.

Zosia had no further questions and moments later found interest in something else. I didn't persist, and so the matter was closed.

At that time, movies for children were rare, but there was a film showing for children in the cinema in Bielsko. I happily bought three tickets and we went to the cinema with excitement.

How disappointed we were when the ticket office lady said that the film was only for older, school-age children and steadfastly refused to let Zosia join the audience. We all were very upset and Zosia was even angry. We comforted her, promising that soon they would show a movie for children of her age.

"But then they won't let grown-ups in the cinema, right? You won't be allowed to go in, right?" she responded with obvious sadness.

We agreed that in that case, we would bring her to the cinema, walk around and then pick her up. it turned out not to be an issue since they weren't showing any movies appropriate for her age anyway and soon we forgot all about it.

It so happened that after the war I again sought the Pogorzelskis' help. During my husband's illness and surgery in Łódź I lived with them until I received permission to stay permanently with my husband in the clinic. Whenever Mom came to visit me from Bielsko, she always stayed with them.

Back in Vilnius, I had to think about Różka. It meant organizing a hide-out. I had no idea how to even begin. I thought that for now I should move out of Rózia's friend's apartment to minimize the risk to her and give her some peace of mind. But I had nowhere to go. I felt terribly lonely. There was no one I could rely on. I was getting weaker physically and mentally and I badly needed moral support.

I decided to get in touch with my friend from the ghetto who'd moved at the time to my room in Kailis on Rydz-Śmigły Street. I went there in the morning and observed some movement around the entrance. The gate and courtyard emptied out once people left for work. But I could see faces in windows, which meant that not everyone had gone. Then a woman from outside walked in after a short conversation with the Jewish guard. She didn't show any papers. A few people went in the same way. I asked one of them who'd just come out how one could enter.

"As usual. If you know the name of anyone living there, you can say you are bringing them some goods."

I tried it. It worked.

My friend Masza was in the house, in my room which she shared with her father, auntie, brother and cousin from Warsaw and her family (8 people altogether). Four bunk beds took up nearly all of the space in the small room.

I didn't talk with Masza for long. I told her about our misfortunes. We decided that I would try to visit her disguised as a peasant she knew who brought food to her family – and then stay illegally for the night. A new routine in my life was created, but didn't last long. I would come to Masza in the afternoon, before people returned from work. I was fat, dressed as a peasant and would easily pass as a Bialers' "country woman." As I walked up the stairs, every now and then a door would open and people would look out to see who'd arrived.

"What are you selling? What have you got to sell?" they asked.

I didn't answer for fear that someone might recognize my voice. They stopped pestering me after a few days.

Still, the doors were left ajar, people gave me unfriendly glances and then I would hear abhorrent comments:

"It's the Bialers' 'goy woman'. She doesn't sell anything to anyone. I don't know how they even pay her."

For a short time I was together with Masza – but we barely talked. Each of us was too afraid to touch on any painful subject, and so much hurt. Sometimes we sat on the bed hugging each other and crying quietly. Sometimes we were simply silent. These short moments gave us some relief. I don't know why but in those moments we didn't have to be consciously or even subconsciously vigilant. Maybe those school years we'd had together somehow protected us from this miserable reality. Later, the rest of the family would return. It became crowded, cramped, stuffy and noisy. They shared their daily experiences, rumors, predictions, talked over minor matters, cooked, ate, and even told jokes which made my hair curl - although they always found them funny.

One day someone shared that a German supervising their work had gotten angry with someone for sawing or cutting something wrong. He was so angry that he grabbed a pair of scissors and cut this Jew's hair in a very unflattering way. The person telling the story was very expressive and mimed what had happened. Everyone laughed.

"If a hairdresser came to me," said Masza's cousin, which caused another bout of laughter, "I'd ask for this hairstyle: here a bald triangle and in the middle a clump of long hair, braided."

The more she talked, the more she went into a trance. Her twisted imagination gave her more and more extreme hairstyles. The audience was almost on the floor with laughter, holding their bellies and wiping tears with their hands. I was petrified. I felt like I was in a psychiatric hospital. I became aware that even with all of my troubles, challenges and misfortunes, I had been living in a more "normal" world. I didn't understand their humor, I couldn't laugh at their jokes.

After supper, the only bathroom for a few dozen people was besieged. This took a long time. Finally, everyone took their place on the bunk beds, two on each bed, and after a brief time all fell silent.

I slept with Masza on the top bunk, but I didn't go to bed at the same time as the others.

I took my shoes off, went out to the long, narrow, windowless corridor and marched for a few hours from one end to the other. I didn't feel nervous or distraught – I was emotionally numb. My head was full of chaos. Thoughts were racing involuntarily, leading me nowhere. The most frequently repeated, unanswerable question was: what to do with Różka? Tears were rolling in abundance down my cheeks –strange, lifeless tears not accompanied by any feelings. I walked like this for three or four hours until physical exhaustion forced me to lie down next to Masza. She wasn't asleep. She wiped my wet face with a towel.

"Sleep now," she said and put her hand on my shoulder like she understood that it was something I needed to do.

I slept only for two or three hours. Early in the morning, the hustle and bustle of dressing, making beds and airing out sheets began. Everyone rushed and pushed others, everyone was in a hurry; they eventually left and there was some peace again. Masza observed the guards through the window. More or less two hours after people left for work the guards changed, and soon after that I left for the city, pretending that I had come in during the first guards' shift, and that I'd quickly done my business and was leaving.

The city was becoming more hostile. My attempts to find a hideout for Rózia felt more like I was banging my head against the wall than a planned and purposeful action. People sent me from one place to another and made vague promises. They never worked out. Perhaps I wasn't the best person to sort it out, I felt inept and was losing confidence with each day. At the end of the day I went to Rózia to tell her what I'd tried to do and to find out if she was all right. Afterwards, I went back to Masza to my nightly walks and few hours of sleep, then did it all over again. I became helpless.

One day Rózia voiced a concern that tormented me for some time.

"Pola, we need to end this. You won't find me a hiding place, it's simply beyond you. I can't stay here for long. My friend doesn't say anything but she's becoming increasingly anxious. I have to go to the ghetto. You can't save me, and you could get in trouble, and there will be no one to help you. Don is not with us anymore. Try to get in contact with someone from the ghetto for me, maybe one of yours or Sierioża's friends."

That night, my march in the corridor was longer than usual. I couldn't come up with any bright ideas and was starting to realize I could not sort things out for Rózia. I got hold of a contact in the ghetto for her. She went in and never came out again alive.

Soon after, the chief of the Kailis police paid Masza a visit.

"This "goy" of yours, that's Pola Komaj, right?" he asked bluntly.

Denial was futile. He was a graduate of Stefan Batory University. He knew me from the Jewish Student Union.

"Today I will turn a blind eye to this, but that's it. I won't put my neck on the line for her and you. I'm warning you," he made himself clear.

Neither of us got any sleep that night. That was the last time in our lives we would meet.

At around eleven o'clock I crossed the Kailis gate for the last time and found myself alone, without a roof over my head, no use to anybody in my once beloved but now indifferent Vilnius. I was completely exhausted and mentally drained. Now, when I had no ambitions, when I was of no use to Mom or Rózia, everything suddenly became unimportant. I stopped caring about "the next step," I started dreaming about the possibility of surrendering to fate, liberating myself from making decisions, taking initiatives or actions. It seemed to me that only the ghetto could provide what I needed. I began to dream of the ghetto as salvation. I recognized that I needed Hilel's help with this; I sent him a message in the ghetto. He set up a meeting in the place I remembered from our previous encounter.

I shared my plan. I begged him, "please, look around for a place to sleep, somewhere to work, and whatever else I need to survive on the other side."

He looked at me from behind thick lenses and didn't speak for some time.

"I won't do it to you," he said decisively. "I am your friend. You won't last long in the ghetto. We got used to it gradually. You won't make it. Besides, Mareczka," (that's what close friends called my mother) "needs you, and you must always be at her disposal. You have to sort something out on that side and keep on living."

I felt like the ground was falling out from under my feet, like my last hope had died. A wave of bitterness and grievance washed over me.

"Don't turn to anyone else with this request," Hilel added like he was reading my thoughts. "I know who you might talk to. I'll warn all of them. You will not enter the ghetto. I won't allow it. In the name of our friendship, I will do everything to prevent it."

We parted in this way and did not meet again for nearly half a century. The next meeting took place in 1988 in Israel, in Tel Aviv, where professor and doctor Chaim Hilel Fryd settled after the war, never to return to Poland.

In the meantime, I was forced again to look for a roof over my head, help and advice.

Aleksander Smilg introduced me to Muszka Fedecka and some others. Through him I met also the third Mr. Frąckiewicz, a reserve officer of the Polish Army who lived with his family at the corner of Archangielska and Wiwulski street, and Maryla and Feliks Wolski.

I don't remember exactly how, but in that time I got a message or heard a rumor that a friend, Szumańska, was working as a doctor at the health center in Szumsko. I knew her from university because she used to borrow books from me. I knew that she was from Łódź and came from a poor PSP[13] family; she definitely wasn't anti-Semitic.

My plan of getting to her and finding employment as a nurse in the center

13   Polish Socialist Party

didn't form a very firm foundation for me to build on. I planned to pose as a runaway from Warsaw, a medical studies trainee. But I was grasping for straws. Above all, I had to get out of Vilnius.

Traveling by train was not advisable for two reasons. Firstly, you never knew who would be in your carriage or compartment, in an enclosed space without any chance of escape. Secondly, at the time, trains traveling east were often targeted and blown up by partisans, making them a risky form of transportation. Another option was getting a lift near the tollhouse on a peasant wagon going in the right direction, which would require a bit of luck.

Meanwhile, I still had to find a place to stay for the next night, and perhaps a few more. Whom should I turn to? Whom could I ask?

I chose Mr. Frąckiewicz, even though this choice made as little sense as any other. He'd seen me at his house probably only twice, why would he risk his and his family's life for me? But if I were to think that way, I would never ask anyone for help – I convinced myself, recalling Aleksander's words: "here people will always be willing to help you but even if they aren't able to, they at least won't put you in danger."

My survival instinct overtook my ethical reservations. I asked Mr. Frąckiewicz to let me stay. He didn't refuse.

I saw his family on a daily basis. Apart from Mr. and Mrs. Frąckiewicz and myself, there was also a boy who was approximately 5 years old, who would sit with us at the table in the evenings. A Jewish boy hidden by them in a city apartment with only one front door, one among many other apartment doors in the stairway.

The boy felt relatively safe, he even fussed over his food, but whenever he heard steps on the stairs, he got up and silently went to his room at the end of the apartment and Mrs. Frąckiewicz moved plates on a table to remove any trace of this fourth guest. After a short time he would come back, and everything would go on as normal. I don't know whether they gave him a signal to return or if he simply came back after enough time had passed. During the night Mr. Frąckiewicz took him out, sometimes asleep, to the yard to get some fresh air.

Hitching a ride on a random wagon turned out to be a difficult task – only a few were going in the right direction and most of them refused to take me. I returned from those adventures like a beaten dog, however those few afternoon hours in the house brought me relief. In one of those evenings, as we were sitting at the table, I heard the unmistakable sound of steps on the stairs. My heart automatically began to pound, but I noticed with surprise that everyone continued to eat their supper calmly and even the little one didn't move. I didn't understand what was happening. I didn't know if I should say something about it and how much the boy understood of this "hide and seek" game. Mr. Frąckiewicz noticed the anxiety in my eyes.

"Is someone coming?" he turned to the boy.

"Don't worry, Granddad. It's only Uncle Stefek!" he replied with a smile.

I think that was the name he used. He was able to discern the steps of the people coming up and down the stairs and recognize whom he should be afraid of. This whole scene lasted no more than a few seconds but was telling. I also met Frąckiewicz's daughter. She was a partisan in the Home Army who one day popped in.

After spending a few hopeless days waiting near the tollhouse, I came back feeling very low, but Mr. Frąckiewicz looked at me joyfully:

"I have good news for you! A neighbor who now lives outside Vilnius, close to Szumsko where he has a small estate, has come for one or two days before returning, and he's promised to take you with him."

"Does he know who I am?" I wondered.

"No, he doesn't, and you don't have to introduce yourself. He'll give you a lift, you'll part and that will be all of your dealings with him. Although, please, don't misunderstand me – he's a very good and reliable man."

I still had to wait a few days for these travel plans. During that time, Mr. Frąckiewicz asked me if I would consider joining the partisans.

"They need doctors," he added, looking at me intently like he wanted to make sure that it was okay to ask this question.

"Yes, I would," I replied after some consideration. "I would go now. Before, I felt responsible for my loved ones. Before, I could only do things for them with Father's instructions. But now? My husband and father are dead. Mom should be safe. Różka is most likely lost. I can't do anything else for them. I'm completely on my own and nothing stands in the way of my taking up the offer."

"Hang on a minute," Mr. Frąckiewicz smiled. "It's not yet an offer. It's only an idea. I would have to get the overall picture. You know, partisan groups differ when it comes to worldview, ideology, attitude to certain matters like potential future collaboration with the Red Army or communist partisans. They even have different attitudes towards Jews. Go to Szumsko and once I have some information for you on this matter, I will make sure to find you and let you know."

Mr. Frąckiewicz also told me something important. He'd seen how parting from Mom was difficult for me – those were the first few weeks of our separate lives and I kept coming back to her in thoughts and conversations. How I was surprised and grateful when Mr. Frąckiewicz unexpectedly said:

"If everything goes according to plan for both of you, and you are able to meet with your mother again, our apartment will be at your disposal if you need a place to meet. Unless everything changes, and things happen that we can't yet imagine."

His offer seemed unrealistic but still gave me a lot of joy.

In Koziełłowszczyzna at the Łokuciewskis'

The day of departure came. We left the bricked bungalow belonging to the Łokuciewski family, a property neighboring the building where Mr. Frąckiewicz lived. Mr. Bronisław was taking me. He was of medium height and slender build. He had warm and kind eyes.

After a short silence, Mr. Bronisław began to tell me about himself, his family, years of his youth. He liked telling stories, he had plenty of them and was good at it. Images passed before my eyes when he spoke of building the Northern-Finish railway: a beautiful land with forest and mountains surrounded by vast waters. The Finns were reliable, trustworthy, incredibly honest; he told me of their cleanliness, saunas and various customs.

"You know, once, early in the morning, I set off with a Finnish guy on horseback. It was cold. I was wearing a wool coat. We had a long journey ahead of us. It got warmer around noon, my coat became heavy and when I took it off and put it on the saddle, it kept sliding off. My companion noticed and said: 'Hang your coat.' 'Where?' – I asked, surprised. 'On a tree. We will be coming back this way.' Indeed, it was such a simple solution which I never would have thought of. But every country has its own customs."

Mr. Bronisław's stories were a nice addition to this journey into the unknown.

"Another thing," he said, "we came off the main road, and on both sides of the path were little poles with boxes on top. Children or adults would come out of their houses, lift the lid, take the letters, sometimes even small parcels, and go back to their houses. 'Mailboxes?' I asked my traveling companion.

'Yes.' 'They are open?' 'Yes. Why would you need to lock them?' Indeed, why would you?

"Around this time I also stayed in Petrograd. What a city it was! And what beautiful women lived there! That's where I met Olga, my wife."

He beamed and it felt like these memories made his soul sing. Suddenly he looked at me.

"Am I boring you?" he asked. "Actually, what's your name?"

"Zosia," I introduced myself with this name for the first time.

"I think I'm boring you, Miss Zosia. I just like to talk about those times and everyone at home knows my stories by heart and doesn't want to listen to me anymore," he smiled to himself.

"No, why? It's all very interesting," I answered honestly.

"Miss Zosia," Mr. Bronisław asked suddenly. "Why are you actually going to Szumsko?"

I explained that I had escaped from Warsaw and that I was a medical student.

"I can't manage in Vilnius – I have no apartment, no job, no Arbeitsschein[14]. Someone told me that I would be able to get a job at the Szumsko Health Center and once I've got work, the rest will sort itself out."

"I propose that you come with me to our place. We have work and food, and a roof over our heads. You'll meet my wife and I'm sure you'll like her because you cannot dislike Olga; you'll help her and somehow, we'll survive the war."

If this conversation had taken place in Vilnius before our departure, if Mr. Frąckiewicz had explained the situation and Mr. Bronisław had kept his invitation, that might have been something else. But now, as we were approaching Szumsko? Mr. Bronisław didn't know whom he was inviting into his home. I couldn't explain it without Mr. Frackiewicz's knowing. I kept refusing but Mr. Bronisław also was stubborn.

"What's the matter? Come with me, you'll spend a few days, a week with us, you'll rest and then if you still want to go to this Szumsko, I will take you there."

It seemed like any further refusal of his hospitability would be suspicious

---

14   work permit (German)

and Mr. Bronisław seemed to be taking offense. I finally agreed to go with him, full of doubts on whether or not I'd made the right decision. We came to Koziełłowszczyzna in the evening. People were busy shredding cabbages. After greetings, introductions and a cup of milk, they went back to work.

Mr. Bronisław went off to take a look at the estate and I, despite Mrs. Olga's protests, joined the work. However, I had to stop after an hour because I got a strong gallbladder colic attack. Naturally, it caused some chaos. Mrs. Olga was terribly concerned. She put me on a bed, pressed something warm on the area of my gallbladder and gave me a hot drink. She covered me up and ordered me to stay quiet.

I don't know what was worse – the pain, or my anxiety about the drama I'd caused. Once I pulled myself together, I decided that from tomorrow I would help Mrs. Olga and leave for Szumsko in a week.

Mrs. Olga got up at dawn and began to make a fire in the kitchen stove. I got up as well. I went to the kitchen to help but it didn't work out as I'd planned. There was nothing else to do with the stove and I didn't know what else I could help with. Mrs. Olga's actions were almost automatic, one quickly led to another. I comforted myself that later in the day or tomorrow I would somehow find a way to be of help.

Mrs. Olga had smoothly combed grey hair and was a beautiful woman with warm, kind eyes. You could feel her inner harmony which made her glow with peace. She worked from dawn till dusk without a hurry but also without rest. The house was spacious with large windows, wooden floors, it was tidy and full of people. Apart from Mrs. Olga and Mr. Bronisław, their two adolescent daughters also lived there (although temporarily), Mr. Bronisław's brother, a widower with three children – Marysia, Lusia and Hubert, who were looked after by Mrs. Olga, and on the other side of the hall, the farm hands' families. Around eight or ten people sat down to the table for meals, and later even more.

The next day, when I took over Mrs. Olga's duty of making a fire in the stove, I completely failed. I couldn't make a fire. I was adamant I would master this art, but the next day was the same. This time Mrs. Olga found a solution.

"Miss Zosia, if you really want to help me, perhaps you could look after the children. I find those lessons very tiring. My poor hearing makes working with them even more difficult. You could also repair their clothes and underwear after I've washed them. It will be a great relief for me and greater help than in the kitchen. Anyway, you can see that the stove is refusing to obey you," she added with a smile. It was decided.

The children took to me without objection, even kindly, and the transition went smoothly.

Peaceful, happy days passed by within the family atmosphere of the Łokuciewski house.

In the morning, everyone sat at the table and stuffed themselves with "stopper" prepared by Mrs. Olga – a thick mash made from brown flour with milk. Mrs. Olga usually asked how people slept and who had dreamed what – I think she believed in the symbolism of dreams and treated them seriously.

After breakfast everyone got busy with their work.

I got into the rhythm of the house. I felt that both Mr. Bronisław and Mrs. Olga liked me. I felt as though I'd snuck into this house and consciously misused their trust. Loyalty towards Mr. Frąckiewicz didn't allow me to explain my situation. I had to do something about it. The Łokuciewskis didn't want to hear about me going to Szumsko.

"What for?" they asked, confused by my persistence. "You can see that you are needed here, you are not a burden to us, it's quiet here, the Germans barely come around – they are scared because it's too far from the main road. Over there you will only have more problems and the authorities to worry about."

It all seemed very reasonable, aside from the fact that they didn't know the truth. I decided to return to Vilnius to talk to Mr. Frąckiewicz and to find out what he thought about the idea.

My stay in Koziełłowszczyzna dragged on. Mr. Bronisław kept saying that he had business to attend to in Vilnius so we could go together, but he didn't seem to be in any hurry. The tension kept rising within me until it reached its height when one morning Mrs. Olga told us about her dream at breakfast.

"I had such a strange dream last night," she said thoughtfully. "I don't know how to explain it. Zosia was in my dream. Her face was covered like a woman from the east and even though I couldn't see it, it seemed to me that she was very pretty. I really wanted to see her face, but every time I attempted to lift the cover, Miss Zosia turned her head. I don't know what this dream means."

I didn't know how to explain the dream either. Perhaps Mrs. Olga had felt or noticed something in my behavior, gestures or facial expressions that made her suspect me of being a Jew? Maybe she was fearful of my presence? What if it was not a dream at all, but a test?

I wasn't afraid of these people, I didn't worry they would harm me, but my double life became nearly unbearable.

Fortunately, Mr. Bronisław at last reached a decision about traveling to Vilnius. I made it to the Frąckiewiczs and finally I could talk openly with someone about my dilemma.

"And that is why you came to Vilnius?" Mr. Frąckiewicz surprised me by asking after listening to my story.

"Well, yes, I had to do something about it."

"Woman, what could you do about it? Can't you see the world we live in? The war is unforgivable, cruel. Is it peaceful there? Safe? Then sit there and don't move until they move you."

"But perhaps I should tell Mr. Łokuciewski that I am Jewish?"

"Miss Zosia, I know them. I'm sure they would keep you. The only difference is that they would no longer sleep soundly. So what for? Go back and stay there as long as you can."

This didn't entirely convince me, nor did it solve my dilemma. But I couldn't find the strength to give up Koziełłowszczyzna and go wandering again. I came back to Koziełłowszczyzna and didn't mention Szumsko again. I tried my best with everything I did. We became even closer. Mrs. Olga and Mr. Bronisław treated me like one of their own, included me in family matters and sought my opinions. Mr. Bronisław once even asked my advice on some financial matters, which I couldn't give at all as the subject was beyond my knowledge and understanding.

But the next serious discussion I held with Mr. Bronisław put me in even more of a problematic situation.

One day, when I was doing lessons with the children as usual, Mr. Bronisław came in, apologized for disturbing us and asked me to let the children go because he wanted to talk to me about something.

A guilty conscience needs no accuser – it shook me to the core. My heart was beating so loudly that I was certain he could hear it. Something was happening. I hoped it was nothing bad. What to do?

The children left. Mr. Bronisław sat at the table, looked at me with piercing eyes like he was trying to guess how I would react. He was very serious but also calm. He cleared his throat like he found it difficult to start the conversation, which I obviously interpreted to mean the worst.

"Miss Zosia," he finally began, "a German-language student from Vilnius has come to us and would like to stay here. Olga and I have talked, we have space for her and if one more person were to share our "stopper," we would be none the poorer. However, Olga said that we should talk to Miss Zosia. What do you think?"

A wave of relief engulfed me.

"What have I got to do with it?" I was surprised to be consulted.

"You see," Mr. Bronisław replied, "she is Jewish. I knew her father very well, he was a reliable merchant who was sadly murdered in the ghetto. I would keep her happily, but Olga says – Miss Zosia needs to know since this would put her in danger. What do you say?"

"Mr. Bronisław, I think that we will manage. We are in the middle of nowhere. Rarely do we have any visitors. The Germans are afraid of this area. We will all be careful."

"That's what I thought, that you wouldn't mind," Mr. Bronisław was relieved.

How bad I felt! Here I was, graciously agreeing to hide a Jew! There was terrible chaos in my head, but there was no time to meditate on it as Mr. Bronisław, after getting my approval, asked me to look after the new guest and to show her around.

"Her name is Mira Brojdes so I think she can keep her name," he mentioned as he was leaving to get her.

Mira was younger than me, but I knew her from the Student Union. When she saw me, she had a beaming smile on her face. As she approached me happily, I stood rigidly, stretched out my hand and introduced myself officially.

"I am Zosia Januszkiewiczówna."

"Mira," she replied, and immediately stopped smiling.

"I know everything," I said, "Mr. Łokuciewski told me."

I introduced Mira to our daily routine and she began to settle in.

One day we saw two Germans approaching the house.

"Miss Zosia, hide Mira and come here," Mr. Bronisław ordered. "If need be, you will probably be better off talking to them in German."

I didn't know whether to laugh or cry. Nothing happened – the Germans changed their minds and didn't even enter the house.

During my last stay in Vilnius I wrote to Mom in Sirvintos and gave her my address. We began to write to each other – pretending to be cousins. I thought about arranging to meet with her.

In the meantime, the days became shorter, the fields emptied, and the winter and Christmas of 1942 were approaching. People were beginning to talk excitedly about Christmas Eve and the children tried to remember lyrics and sang some carols. One day, they came up with the idea that I would teach them a new Christmas carol. I had nothing. I didn't even know the lyrics to the most popular Christmas carols which, if you lived in Poland, you would surely know. I tried to avoid it as best I could, blaming poor memory. But at the same time I decided to learn them from the children so that at least my ignorance wouldn't be exposed.

Every day in the evening, as they were just about to sing, I got an awful migraine, lay down with a hot wet towel on my forehead and waited "for the pain to pass," whilst in fact I was listening carefully to the words of the carols and committing them to memory. But still, I couldn't "remember" any others.

Not knowing the customs and rituals also made me anxious about the forthcoming holidays. I knew that everyone shared Christmas wafers, but when did you do it? How much of the wafer were you supposed to take? What was the correct order of doing things? Does everyone share with everyone? Perhaps there are strict rules.

All of this occupied my mind and made me anxious. I wished for Christmas to be over.

Christmas Eve came. The big table was covered with a white linen and Mrs. Olga put a selection of Christmas dishes on it with kutia at the center. The room was very bright. Everyone looked neat, tidy, and refreshed from their afternoon naps.

Mrs. Olga arranged the seating, placing me on one side of Mr. Bronisław and herself on the other side. I hoped that Mr. Bronisław would share the wafer with Mrs. Olga first so that I could watch, make notes, and then all would be okay. How petrified I was when Mr. Bronisław took the wafer off the plate and turned to me first as I was his guest. I tried to resist, claiming that I wasn't a guest anymore and that Mrs. Olga should be prioritized above me. But Mr. Bronisław didn't yield and I, unsure how sound my argument was, surrendered, broke a bit of the wafer off and following Mr. Bronisław's lead, put it in my mouth. Totally exhausted by the experience, I kept watching how others shared the wafer lege artis[15].

Once I was certain I hadn't made a blunder, I calmed down and joyfully joined in this pleasant atmosphere of a holiday evening and hungrily ate what Mrs. Olga had magically conjured up for the evening.

Suddenly, we heard a quiet knock on the window. There was complete silence. We listened. The knocking continued. Mira went to the cellar, I followed to lock her in, and Mr. Bronisław went to the front door.

"Who is it?" Mr. Bronisław asked.

"Does Mr. Bronisław Łokuciewski live here?" replied an unfamiliar voice in Russian.

"Yes."

"Please, let me in, I am the son of…" the voice from behind the door mentioned the name of a laborer who used to work for Mr. Bronisław years ago.

A young boy, approximately nineteen years old, tall, exhausted and dressed in ragged clothes came in. His name was Danilo and when he'd gone off to war, he was told by his father that if something bad were to happen

---

15   "complying with the law" (Latin)

to him in eastern Poland, he should look for Bronisław Łokuciewski who would be sure to help him. Once his regiment was scattered across Vilnius and the surrounding area, he looked for Bronisław Łokuciewski's estate. He reached Koziełłowszczyzna on Christmas Eve and stayed with us as the third "war" member of the family.

Soon after this, three people - Mr. Bronisław's brother, his nephew and Danilo – fell ill with typhoid fever. I had no more time for lessons – I was too busy nursing the sick. Mrs. Olga, in addition to her duties, felt responsible for protecting me from infection. Every evening when I could barely stand up from exhaustion and my only wish was to lie down in my clothes, Mrs. Olga filled a large bowl with warm water, ordered me to take all of my clothes off and to wash thoroughly from head to toe while she boiled all my clothes in a pot. Afterwards, she gave me something warm to drink and put me to bed. With such devoted care, I truly felt more or less recovered by the next morning.

Nursing Danilo was the most difficult as he became so attached to me during his illness that he didn't want to stay alone in a room for even a moment and didn't want anyone but me with him. I could have a break from the others, once I'd sorted them out, fed them, made their beds and aired their rooms, but Danilo required my constant care. Although truth be told, he was the most unwell. Besides, it seemed that my presence gave him a sense of security. But still, in contrast to the others, this wasn't his home. Once I'd finished doing all that needed my attention, he would ask me to moisten his very chapped lips.

"Drink, drink, drink. Zosia, drink," he constantly asked in a loud, begging whisper.

Dur to his constant sweating, his wet shirt needed to be changed a few times a day. He didn't have enough strength to sit up and as he was large and heavy, lifting him up required a lot of effort from me. During his brief naps, I sneaked out quietly to the kitchen to sit down for a bit or to drink something but in no time I would hear his petrified whisper again, interrupted by his irregular breathing: "Zosia, Zosia, Zosia." Mrs. Olga's persuasion didn't help at all.

"Danilo, let Zosia catch her breath. She is just taking a break," she spoke to him in Russian.

"Ok, let her breathe," he looked carefully at Mrs. Olga and soon after we would hear his whispers again, "Zosia, Zosia, drink."

But this all turned out to be a trifle in comparison with the urinary retention he later contracted. We couldn't take him to hospital, nor could we bring him help – a boy of military age, Russian, who couldn't speak any other language, had no documents and could become delirious with high fever – who knew what he might say. I could feel with my hand, when examining him, that his bladder was getting bigger by the minute. Danilo became more restless, fidgeting in bed, moaning loudly. What to do?

"Mr. Bronisław, we must get a catheter," I said.

"And who will fit it?"

"I will."

"Do you know how?" he asked, uncertain.

"Yes."

However, I was full of doubts. I'd only done it a few times for women and once for a man and even that was a few years ago. I frantically tried to remember how to do it. What complications could I cause if it was not inserted properly?

I had no answers to my many questions.

Mr. Bronisław brought a few catheters that he'd borrowed from the health center. I threw them into boiling water and once they were sterilized, I got to work. The whole house stopped as I worked. Then, the urine began flowing. Danilo stopped howling and before I even realized what had happened, he was embracing me, kissing my face all over. As "a reward", I became even more needed, utterly irreplaceable, and he wouldn't let me leave the room even for a moment.

His young, strong body overcame the illness. I began to sit him up in bed. Soon he would be able to try walking again. At the same time I became visibly weaker, perhaps because I'd stopped being anxious about his survival. Each movement felt like a huge effort and the evening baths were like torture, even though I knew that Mrs. Olga barely had the strength to organize them.

Danilo became more conscious of what was going on around him. Mrs. Olga managed to get him to rest after dinner, which gave me a break too. After introducing an afternoon nap, we all began to get back to a more balanced life.

Learning to walk again required a lot of effort from both Danilo and me. He was very weak and his first steps, for both of us, required Herculean effort. I stood him up next to the bed on his wobbly legs and supported him around the waist (I was much shorter than he was), and with the order "go," he let go of the handrail on the bed, shifting his body weight onto my shoulder and that's how we tried to walk. Starting with one step, each day we added one more. During those first few days of "walking", I must have been more tired than him, and after each attempt I checked if my spine was all right considering how much weight he placed on my shoulders. But after many trials, he became stronger and would lean on my shoulder less and less, so eventually we managed well. Mrs. Olga, who always knew how to look after each of us – when to feed and how to ensure we slept, kept our spirits up and bodies healthy. The others who were sick got through the illness without any complications.

The only benefit of typhus was that it kept the Germans away. The occupation authorities had ordered homes to be marked with white paper crosses stuck to the windows if they housed people sick with typhus, and the Germans thankfully steered clear of those houses.

After my last visit to Vilnius I would get letters from Mom from time to time. I waited for those letters with such noticeable impatience that one day, feeling sad after not having received any word, Mrs. Olga asked me why I was so attached to my cousin. I told her that I'd lost my mother when I was young, and that this cousin had raised me. She was very good to me, and I missed her terribly. So, when the opportunity arose to go to Vilnius with Mr. Bronisław, it seemed natural that I would want to meet my cousin. I can't remember any of the details of the meeting, only that it happened. We met at Mr. Frąckiewicz's house. We finally saw each other for the first time after a long separation. Despite our correspondence and the news that Mima Pogorzelska passed on to me when she came to Vilnius, we didn't know much about each other. In some ways what we knew was enough, because we knew that we were alive and that we were among people who were not only keeping us safe, but were also kind and attached to us, and that we respected and liked them. In this regard, Mom lived in luxury as she didn't have to pretend anything with the Pogorzelskis. But my insincerity towards the Łokuciewskis weighed on my heart.

All I can say about our meeting is that our joy was tainted by the pain of our loss and the prospect of parting again. There was longing in our eyes, but we shared a huge gratitude towards Mr. Frąckiewicz who in such hard times understood that 'man cannot live by bread alone.'

Still, it wasn't plain sailing. Mom had fallen and broken her arm. I vaguely remember taking her to a surgeon's house. It was a wealthy villa. The surgeon received us without enthusiasm, which didn't surprise us as we'd told him that we were doctors and Jewish; however he didn't refuse to help and fitted her with a cast. A few days later, Mom went back to Sirvintos and then a few days after that I was scheduled to return with Mr. Bronisław to Koziełłowszczyzna.

How surprised I was when, a day before our departure, Mr. Frąckiewicz told me I probably shouldn't go back there.

"Koziełłowszczyzna was taken by a partisan group with the intention of turning it into a hospital," He warned me.

"Well, that works out perfectly. I'll be of use."

"I'm not sure whether they will accept you," he said. "It's difficult to explain things in such circumstances. It's probably better not to go back."

"And what shall I say to Mr. Bronisław?"

"Nothing. Just don't see him before his departure and I'll say that you had to go somewhere out of Vilnius and that I don't know when you will be back. There's not much point in waiting."

It was very hard for me to follow his advice. How could I simply disappear? Without explanation? Without thanking them? They didn't deserve that.

But I behaved in the same way as I had done towards Nikołaj Aleksandrowicz.

It wasn't until 1946 that I saw Mrs. Olga again in Łódź. I went there on a business trip. Completely by accident I found out from someone that Mrs. Olga was there with the children and went to the address I had been given.

The meeting was very moving. We embraced and kissed affectionately.

"Miss Zosia, I'm so happy to see you," Mrs. Olga kept saying.

"Mrs. Olga, I'm not Zosia, I'm Pola Komaj," I interjected.

"I don't care. The most important thing is that you are alive and that we have reunited," she replied.

After that, our friendship lasted until Mrs. Olga's death. To this day I've kept some of her letters which reflected to some degree the nature of our post-war friendship.

My Lithuanian Family

So, I was back in Vilnius once more, back with the Frąckiewiczes and once again, unsure what to do.

One day by pure chance I met Marysia Rzeuska, a friend of my husband's from his philosophy seminars (in addition to his medical studies he also studied philosophy). I knew her from Sierioża's stories as someone who had integrity, but who could be almost aggressive and blunt in wanting to prove that she was right about everything. Later, I met her in person – she was sickly, always having problems with her heart and lungs – she used to come to Sierioża for intravenous injections which had just become more common. Only a doctor could administer medication intravenously but at that time there was not a wide range of medicines available. They usually used calcium which gave a sense of warmth during injection and this amazing side effect raised people's hopes of recovery. These "hot injections" were very popular.

Marysia was prescribed those injections by a doctor and Sierioża had administered them. Afterwards, she usually stayed for tea or supper to chat. However, our relationship wasn't very close or intimate. We were just good acquaintances.

I bumped into Marysia when I was in Vilnius. She already knew my situation and we agreed that I would visit her.

She lived as a lodger at some professor's house, on Szeptycki Street, in a room so small that it was difficult to fit a second person in. The professor's apartment was very big and uncomfortably wealthy for a person in a situation like mine. There was no one at home besides Marysia – perhaps she'd set this time for our meeting intentionally? She offered me tea and said that she didn't have anything yet she could help me with but that perhaps something would turn up. She suggested a visit to her friends who were willing to help me with my problems.

That's how I met the Charytonow ladies.

The Charytonow family lived in their own bungalow at the edge of the forest, separated from it only by a forest road. Mr. Charytonow wasn't at home, only Grandma Charytonow, his mother, and Mrs. Charytonow – his wife, were there. I'd been to their house several times; however, I'd never met Mr. Charytonow. Once, Grandma said casually: "My son is gone again. Maybe it's better. He likes to drink."

Straight away you could feel that Grandma ran the house. Still, she wasn't a dictator who reigned with an iron fist. She gained authority through her endearing goodness, boundless energy and vitality, initiative and caring. You didn't have to know her long to see it quite clearly. She was of medium height and despite being overweight, was still very active. She had dark hair, smoothly combed over her round head which sat right on top of her torso, completely concealing her neck; her kindly smiling round face also had black eyes full of goodness. Her whole body seemed to be round.

While she was hosting us, she was constantly on the move – she looked in a pot in a kitchen, watered plants, offered tea and jam while talking about preserves for winter. My visit was short, because Grandma Chary-tonow suggested I go with her without delay to a lady who could offer me temporary accommodation.

Marysia stayed and Grandma and I set off. The journey was short because the apartment was located at Wielka Pohulanka Street, just up the hill in a good house. A young woman in her thirties opened the door and we followed her to the kitchen.

"How are you doing, Mrs. Marysia?" Grandma greeted her. "Have you got something good and inexpensive for me? Maybe a piece of meat? But I haven't introduced my acquaintance – Miss Zosia is an escapee from Warsaw, a medical student, she's just come to Vilnius. And how are you managing, Mrs. Marysia? Are the children well?"

"They are healthy, but it's a struggle with them. I have no one to leave them at home with and my wares will not come to me on their own. I have to go and find them, haggle, and then bring them back. And I can't do that with one child in my arms and another in a stroller, but I can't leave them at home alone, they are too small."

"Exactly. I was just thinking that until miss Zosia gets settled, perhaps she could live with you for a bit and look after the children to help you. And, you know, Zosia would be happy just with bed and board, you wouldn't even have to pay her."

Mrs. Marysia looked at me shyly; she didn't look like a lady accustomed to hiring servants.

"Gladly, if it suits Miss Zosia."

This was how Grandma Charytonow did business. Then, she went home, leaving me with Mrs. Marysia.

"I'll show you the apartment," Mrs. Marysia said shyly and showed me around.

The hall led to a spacious room with a big window and a balcony door. There was also a full-length standing mirror.

A quarter of the room was taken up by a piano. Nothing else. It was obvious that this room was not in use and was treated only as a hallway. From this room, two sets of doors led into two other rooms. Their use was very clear. One of them, just slightly smaller than the salon/corridor, was used as a storage room for the goods traded by Mrs. Marysia. On the floor were barrels, bags full of sugar, salt, hulled grains, meat and dry sausage, none in very large amounts.

The next room, the smallest, served as the living room. In it was a large, framed metal bed with four shiny spheres, one in each corner, a child's bed where the older boy slept and a stroller for the younger one. A medium-sized table with two chairs completed the furnishing.

There was also a bathroom with a bathtub and toilet.

When we circled back into the kitchen, Mrs. Marysia looked at me with uncertainty.

"But I will be embarrassed telling you what to do," she said, "because I am a simple woman and you are educated."

"You can tell me now what you would like me to do and I will try my best to do it, that way you won't have to repeat yourself – and if I forget or miss anything, you should tell me."

She had an anxious look about her, so I tried to comfort her.

"Please, don't worry. You'll see, everything will be fine."

In the meantime, the boys let us know from the other room that they were awake. I went into their room with Mrs. Marysia. They looked at me with vague curiosity. When Mrs. Marysia went back to the kitchen, I began to dress them, and they didn't resist. It was a clear achievement when the older one, Waldek, after lacing up his shoes, climbed abruptly onto my lap, put his elbows on the table and made it clear that he expected a meal. The younger one was easy – he was almost a year old and my attempts to communicate in his own language with warmth, hugs, and smiles were good enough. Their approval lifted my spirits.

Mrs. Marysia gave us dinner. I don't know why but I felt the dinner was more like a special occasion. I suspected that they usually just ate in the kitchen – partially sitting, partially standing or even walking around.

Later, I sat with the boys again. Mrs. Marysia tidied up the kitchen and then said that she was going shopping. In the evening, after bath time we put the boys to bed and rested at the table. We didn't have much to talk about and there was only one book to read – "Trędowata." Mrs. Marysia offered me the first part of the book as she was already reading the second half.

Since there was nothing else to do, I scanned my part of 'Trędowata', thinking about the events of the day. Marysia was fully immersed in her reading.

I was tired and my spine was sore from all the sitting down but there was no hint of going to sleep. When it got very late and both Mrs. Marysia and I looked very sleepy, I decided to take initiative.

"I guess we should go to bed. Do the boys wake up early?"

"Yes, early."

"Right, then we should not be tired."

She got up and looked unsure, like she was lost in thought, and began to prepare two bedding arrangements: one on the bed, the other on the floor.

"I'll sleep here," she said, "I have only one bed."

Other than sleeping together in one bed, there was no other option. I didn't want to agree to her sleeping on the floor, but she wouldn't even entertain the thought of me sleeping there.

Marysia was very good to me and willing to share everything she had. Even when she lit a cigarette, she would offer me one.

However, as the days passed by, some problems began to emerge. There was no man in the house, I didn't know who the boys' father was and it was something we never talked about.

But soon after I moved in, a man appeared, one much older than she was. He brought some presents, was warmly received and stayed for a few days.

I had to give up the bed and the room. I moved with a duvet to the bathroom and this would have been comfortable enough if it weren't for one small detail. The tap dripped slowly but consistently onto the duvet and my legs. No matter what I did, I couldn't stop the leak. Still, it was something I could live with and after the man left, I went back to the bedroom with Marysia, who was a bit embarrassed by the whole situation and felt she owed me an explanation. She told me that the man was a Lithuanian, an engineer from Kaunas where he had a house, wife and adolescent children. But this was his second home as he was the boys' father, too, and came now and again for a few days bringing financial help.

My presence didn't mean anything to him, he was not interested in me.

After this visit, there was candy and other sweets at home. I found out that on such occasions, Mrs. Marysia usually invited a few female neighbors for tea.

So, I was destined to take part in a social meeting which I wasn't happy about. I was very surprised when Mrs. Marysia was getting ready for the party and said to me:

"I told my friends that you came from Lithuania, and you are my sister-in-law. Please, don't betray yourself."

"Why did you tell them that?" I replied, afraid of blowing my cover as I didn't know Lithuanian, Kaunas, nor 'my family'.

"They are simple women. If they thought you worked for me, they might be bad or rude towards you. But it'll be different with family, especially coming from my husband's side."

Soon, my connections with Mrs. Marysia's family would become even stronger. The business was not going well, and the reason was probably very simple – counting and trading were not her strengths. There were fewer goods and clients and more arguments with customers, especially with those regulars for whom she agreed to delayed payments. Paying rent for such a large apartment in a good area became a struggle. Mrs. Marysia started to look for a smaller flat and her brother – a Lithuanian policeman – helped her. Mrs. Marysia stuck to the story of my connection to her husband's family and my coming from Lithuania to help her.

I don't know how, but the fact that her brother had never met me before and my lack of knowledge of the Lithuanian language seemed to be problematic only to me.

We moved from Wielka Pohulanka to a two-bedroom flat on Wiwulska Street. Mrs. Marysia's brother lived above us with his wife, whom he beat regularly and mercilessly. We listened downstairs to the sounds of these domestic scenes with tight hearts.

Mrs. Marysia's "business" was diminishing with each day. She couldn't acquire more goods as she didn't have the money to buy them; we ate through our provisions carefully until all we could only eat was semolina with water. Soon we were eating it without salt as well, after Mrs. Marysia, dreading the humiliation, stopped asking to borrow it from the neighbors. Obviously, there was no money for cigarettes. However, if the neighbors offered her some, she would bring me either a cigarette butt or a broken piece of one. You could see Mrs. Marysia's character in this way – she loved her husband unconditionally, even though he didn't really care about his second family; she loved her boys and I never observed her treating them as a burden; she became my friend and shared with me everything she had. But I began to feel guilty about eating the children's food in the same way I'd felt guilty at Mr. Hipolit's in the springtime.

Grandma Charytonow visited us sometimes at Wielka Pohulanka and also at the new place and she was aware of our situation.

The spring of 1943 came. On May 15th, in the early morning, a bell rang and a huge bunch of fragrant lilacs slipped through the door with Grandma Charytonow right behind it.

"Good morning, Miss Zosia. I wanted to be the first to wish you a happy name day and to kiss you. Mrs. Marysia, can you take these flowers, I can barely hold onto them." After she'd given the flowers to Marysia, she embraced me. "I have some time, shall we go to church?" and, kissing me, she whispered: "I was afraid you'd forget about your name day. I need to talk to you."

Apart from the flowers, there was also cake and tea. We had a name day party and went with Grandma to church. The neighborhood was quiet, with only a few pedestrians scattered about, and the weather was nice, so we walked and talked.

I found out from Grandma Charytonow that Marysia Rzeuska wanted to see me. There was a family that was going to be leasing a piece of land and a summer house outside the city. They had three boys and needed someone to look after them. They knew the truth and were willing to take me in but wanted to first meet and talk about it.

The Święcickis lived near Maria Rzeuska. There was Ada – a painter, Józef – a journalist, and their three boys.

Summer at Lake Galve, 1943

The Święcickis had already thought of everything – their idea was that they would place an advertisement in the newspaper looking for someone to look after the children in exchange for bed and board. I was meant to be the person responding to this advertisement. They were going to keep it up just in case. Aside from that, they knew nothing about me.

The summer house was by the lake. A large wooden one-story house surrounded by fields, situated near the lake which was surrounded by bushes and with a lovely path that ran parallel to the shore. The shore was quite high in places and completely flat in others, so the path went up and down accordingly. Only the areas with bushes offered a pleasant coolness on hot days.

Apart from Mrs. Ada, the painter and Mr. Józef, the journalist, their children and me, there was also a seamstress. Everything was well organized: Mrs. Ada and Mr. Józef had their own things to do; they were responsible for leasing the land and house and also for the food supply. Mrs. Ada cooked. After all, there were seven of us to feed. My main duty was looking after the boys, their education, development and hygiene. In my free time I helped Mrs. Ada in the kitchen, especially towards the end of the week when she needed to cook extra for Sunday guests. Our main visitors were Mr. Józef's parents and Mrs. Ada's sister with her fiancé. The seamstress repaired bedding, underwear and clothes and she had her hands full. The joint leaseholder often came around in the evenings, either for business or just to have a chat.

The boys, Maciek, Piotruś and Giguś, were lovely but all looked very different and had distinct characters to match. The eldest, 9-year-old Maciek, had brown hair and was well-built. He had a very rich imagination and was happy to spend time alone in an imaginary world with his two main passions: composing and sailing; this was also reflected in real life. Because Maciek was older and was able to wash his own feet before bed, I would pour water into a bowl and give him soap and a towel to wash himself while I got Piotruś and Giga ready for bed. At first, I found it irritating returning to the bowl to empty and clean it, only to find him still in the same position, daydreaming with two legs in the bowl or sometimes with one leg washed and out of the bowl whilst the other one was still in the cold water. Although I later got used to this.

"Maciek, you should be ashamed. Piotruś and Giguś are already in bed after their bath, and you've only managed to wash one foot!"

"It's because I was making up a song."

"Couldn't you do that during the day and not now?"

"Now it's quiet. You know, Miss Zosia, I will be a composer when I grow up."

"I'm sure it's possible, but even a composer needs to wash his feet," I brought him back to reality.

He looked at me absent-minded. My arguments only touched the surface of his consciousness. His facial expression helpless and bored, he finished carelessly washing and went to bed.

Maciek Święcicki later became a contemporary music composer; unfortunately, he is not alive today.

His passion for sailing was more of a problem. There was no sailboat on the lake and the fishing boat and kayak could only be used with an adult's supervision. So whenever Maciek was overwhelmed by an irresistible desire for sailing, he did it in a room on the first floor. He moved chairs, stools and other small pieces of furniture and joined them together with ropes for drying laundry, strings and wires. An important part of the process involved a brush, a broom, sometimes even a fireplace poker and, of course, bedsheets. Once I managed to stand unnoticed at the door to observe his "sailing." His body movement illustrated abrupt tilts, muscle tension during strong winds and then total relaxation during windless weather.

Mrs. Ada had a very good intuitive approach to raising the boys and had a good relationship with them. After I shared my observations of Maciek's sailing, we agreed to allow him to do it, even though it meant occasionally sacrificing a table leg or bedsheet.

Seven-year-old Piotruś was very different from Maciek and five-year-old Giga both in appearance and mentality. He was of a delicate and fragile build. He had thin, light, curly hair. His face was brightened by his trusting, light-blue eyes. He was neurasthenic and sentimental, always needing the assurance of being loved, as though Maciek's indifference and Giga's aggression left him feeling slightly insecure. He was easy to relate to and shared his feelings, dreams and thoughts openly and gladly. Quickly, we became close and serious friends.

That first evening at the summer house Mrs. Ada told me that Piotruś sometimes wet the bed at night and that he was embarrassed about it and would be very distressed if anyone mentioned it.

In the morning, when I noticed that he was awake, I asked him to get up, but Piotruś pulled the covers up to his chin and his eyes shone with tears.

"Miss Zosia, I had an accident," he said in a half-whisper.

"What accident?" I asked casually, trying not to make a big deal out of it.

"I weed in my bed. But I didn't know. I was asleep."

"That's nothing bad. It could happen to anyone," I tried to minimize his shame.

"But I'm embarrassed!"

"You know what? Nobody needs to know about it. I'll wash the bedding in a minute, we'll hang it in the loft so no one will see it and it will be dry by the evening."

"And it won't smell bad?"

"Of course not."

We bonded over this shared secret. I hid it well from the other boys and Mrs. Ada and Mr. Józef pretended they knew nothing.

In the evening, when we brought down the fresh and scented bedding, Piotruś, standing on the bed, hugged me.

"What if it happens again?" he whispered in my ear.

"Nothing. But it doesn't have to happen every night, right? You'll go wee before bed and later when I go to bed I'll wake you up again, and maybe nothing will happen at all."

"All right," Piotruś said, happy with this plan.

For the next few days we stuck to the plan, and soon saw results. "Accidents" still occurred from time to time but less often, and Piotruś admired me even more. Once, I was making him breakfast and he was already outside. When I came into the room where we ate and where my bed was, I saw that it was covered in pieces of grass and flowers without stems. I wasn't sure what was going on until I saw Piotruś's radiant face.

"I left early," he said, coming up to me, "to bring you flowers. Aren't they pretty?"

"Very pretty! And I'm so pleased that you brought them for me."

I stooped down to give him a kiss and thank him but he threw his arms around my neck.

"Because I love you," he said quietly in my ear.

"Me too. Very much."

Piotruś used to have lovely dreams about the future. Once I went to the village to get eggs and took him with me. We were walking on a narrow path alongside the lake. It was sunny, and the water was calm.

Swallows flying high above us were a sign of continued good weather. Piotruś was walking ahead and shared his observations.

"Miss Zosia, you know what?" he said thoughtfully, "when the war is over and you are an old lady, I will buy you a comfortable armchair, and then you will sit in the chair and I will come and play droughts with you. Is that okay?"

Even though I was only 28 years old and it was hard to imagine the end of the war or being 'an old lady', I had to accept this plan as Piotruś was full of love and goodness.

Even so, he was quite a sensitive child. He was easily offended by teasing or mockery and could also be stubborn. Often when the weather was bad the boys sat next to me and I read to them out loud. Once I read a poem, probably by Brzechwa.

Dwarfs from all the cities
Gathered in the forest
The order of gathering was as follows:
Firstly, where crayfish hibernate,
Secondly...
Thirdly...
Fourthly...

And here instead of saying "why children are stubborn," I said, "why Piotruś is stubborn." Piotruś's neck, ears and face became red and tears glimmered in his eyes.

"Miss Zosia, how could you? It doesn't say that!" Piotruś's tone was reproachful.

I knew that I'd upset him and I felt sorry. I learned something at that moment. I could get through to Piotruś in a different way – through affection, warmth, closeness.

Giguś was the exact opposite of Piotruś – he had a strong, masculine build, was physically active, to the point, reasonable, and as the youngest, often thought he was treated unfairly when it came to sharing, fun or privileges. As a result, and just in case, he employed a defensive-offensive attitude which usually turned out badly for Piotruś. All of Giguś's complaints and accusations began with these words:

"It's because I am the smallest (the youngest, the weakest), Miss Zosia, isn't it?"

He certainly didn't let the others take advantage of him.

All three of them were fascinated with cutting little boats out of tree bark and sailing them on the water. This meant that knives were often left scattered all over the place and sometimes it was hard to find even one knife in the kitchen. One day, I ruled that only one knife would be used for cutting boats and each of the boys would take turns using it for a limited amount of time. This caused lots of arguments and the rule was deemed to be unfair. Giguś, as the youngest, thought that he was being treated unfairly, and objected most profusely. He claimed and used the shared knife for the longest time. Maciek treated him as a child and generously shared his knife time with him whilst Piotruś let him use it for longer as he didn't like conflict and perhaps he was a bit afraid of him too.

I felt good in this house. I got on very well with Mrs. Ada and we liked each other. I loved the boys and they fascinated me. I didn't have much to do with the seamstress. I only felt anxious whenever rumors circled about Germans nearby. She hid herself in the loft and asked me to lock her up there and put something in front of the door to camouflage it. I thought that I was in the most danger, but I had to pretend that it was okay, and to give an impression of security. Obviously, I couldn't explain anything at that time.

After the war, I met her on a street in Vilnius. As we were reminiscing about the old days, I found out that she was Jewish too – and so it all became clear.

The co-leaseholder of the Święcickis was the cause of the most anxiety among us. He often came in the evenings, bringing news from the city which often included stories about the Jews and the ghetto. I always had the impression he was carefully watching me when he talked. But I don't know if this was real or imagined and I had no choice but to take part in these conversations.

One day, Mrs. Ada and Mr. Józef went to Vilnius with the intention of returning late in the evening. They didn't return alone. They brought with them a Jewish boy who had been rescued from the ghetto several days earlier. He was of similar age to "our" boys, but he was so different. His skin was pale yellow, and his eyes were black and constantly terrified. He moved slowly, like an old man, and he was scrawny and timid.

Mrs. Ada said, "we agreed to take him and didn't know what he would look like, but we had no choice when we saw him. He is the son of a doctor…" and she told us his name.

The first order of business was to feed him and give him a sense of security. It wasn't easy. It was clear that he'd been through some bad experiences. He appeared so much more mature in comparison to his stronger and healthier peers whose problems revolved around boats made from tree bark.

Mrs. Ada could not keep him concealed and soon decided to reveal him. Their main concern was the co-leaseholder.

One evening when their partner was dining with us, Mrs. Ada brought the boy in and said:

"This is my friends' son from the city. They are very poor and the boy started to become ill from lack of food; I brought him here so he could get some fresh air and eat better."

The man's face betrayed disbelief. He gave the boy a piercing look before shifting to stare at me as though trying to find a connection or familiarity between us. I was growing more and more restless. I started to bustle around in the kitchen to mask my feelings and fear. The more rattled we appeared, the more his conviction grew.

"Is this your son? He is so pale, like a little Jew from the ghetto," he turned to me unexpectedly.

"Of course not," I snorted. "I am not married."

"Well, sometimes it happens to the unmarried ones," he replied and smiled at me knowingly.

"But it didn't happen to me."

"Strange. You are worth a sin."

He had never allowed himself before to talk in such a familiar manner – he must have been feeling very confident. He stayed for quite a long time. When he finally left, we were all left exhausted and anxious. A sense of danger loomed. Early in the morning, the Święcickis left and took the boy with them, certain that he would not be able to adapt to his new reality quickly enough so as not to put all of our lives at serious risk.

But this hasty decision hadn't been thought through well and made the co-leaseholder even more suspicious of the Święcickis' home. His visits increased. He would often sit next to me and tell me horrific stories about selections and executions in the ghetto and at Ponary, all the while watching me carefully. I had to take this news calmly and with interest. The worst part was the questions he would ask from time to time.

"Who knows if they will manage to kill them all? There are still lots of them. They bring them from small towns and they are like fleas. What do you think? Will they make it?"

"What do I know?" I answered, indifferently, barely in control of my emotions. I felt my heart pounding, my breathing accelerated and I had an irresistible desire to spit in his face or even punch him, even though I had never done anything like that in my life.

His game of cat and mouse with me lasted until the end of my stay in the countryside. It was a time of constant anxiety, uncertainty and tension for me.

That summer would hold many a challenging experience.

Some few weeks later, the Święcickis again brought a Jewish woman of similar age to me to the countryside. She wasn't in as bad a condition as the little boy had been. She was dressed neatly and didn't have a particularly Semitic face. They introduced her as a Conservatory graduate, a pianist and a member of the Maccabi sport club who practiced swimming and kayaking. Until this day I don't know what she knew about me. I can't remember if she had any chores in the house, I assume she was there under the guise of a friend who had come for a summer break. We spent a lot of time together.

It was now the second half of summer. A heatwave descended on us. I spent a lot of time with the boys by the lake where they never got bored and always had something to amuse them, what with making and putting little boats on the water, skipping stones, wading through the water or listening to me reading in the fishing boat. We would return to the house for dinner and then go back to our boat. The heat was unbearable and lasted for many days. We tried to cool ourselves down by pouring water over our heads, however relief was brief.

Our new lodger, Mrs. Z., went in the water every now and again to swim, which we were obviously very envious about. She tried to teach the boys how to swim close to the shore. Maciek was not interested, and Piotruś was afraid to even put his head under, but Giguś was very eager to learn and had no fear of the water.

One day, Mrs. Z. suggested that we go kayaking. I objected, arguing that she was the only one who could swim. I could only stay in water for a little bit. Giguś was thrilled, but Piotruś didn't want to do it. Mrs. Z. looked at the upside-down kayak, turned it over, dragged it out of the bushes, paddled out some and came back to us.

"Come on, I'll take you out for a bit, just here close to the shore," she offered. "It's shallow here and not dangerous."

I didn't agree but Giguś was insistent. She lifted him into the kayak, they paddled off for a little while, staying close, and returned. Giguś was delighted but wanted more. Mrs. Z. asked me to join them.

"This kayak is for two adults, but Giga and Piotruś could easily come with us. I promise I know what I'm doing. After all, I am a member of the Maccabi club."

She was sitting in the front seat and Giga was in the back one.

"Mrs. Zosia, come on, let's go. Piotrek, you too, get in," he urged his brother.

Piotruś wasn't interested. Maybe he was afraid. At any rate, he did not want to get in the kayak. Maciek wasn't with us. Unfortunately, I succumbed. I took the back seat, Giga sat between my legs and tried to convince Piotruś to get in.

"You're sure you don't want to join us, Piotruś? Just stay here and play in the fishing boat and we'll be back soon, okay?" I asked but he objected.

"You are older than me and such a coward!" Giga was annoyed.

Piotruś approached the kayak slowly.

"Sit in front of me," Mrs. Z. encouraged him. "You'll see how nice this will be." She helped Piotruś into the kayak and hugged him. "You see, it's fine. Let's go."

The water was perfectly still, not even one ripple. I had a paddle. We left the shore and floated alongside the bushes.

Not long after we'd left, I suddenly started to feel water rising quickly underneath me and before I could say a word, we were all in the lake.

Giguś held tightly onto my neck.

"Giguś, don't hold me so tight! And move your legs like a frog to keep us afloat!"

"All right," he replied and followed my instructions.

Mrs. Z. was somehow quite far from us and she seemed to be swimming in a strange way, holding and pushing Piotruś in front of her. The kayak was upside down and had drifted far away. In my panic, the shore seemed far away and empty. I saw Mrs. Z. dive a few times, still holding Piotruś by his hair.

"Giguś, we need to call for help, but hold on to me the whole time and keep moving your legs!" and we started to shout, "Help! Help!"

An older man appeared on a hill, alerted by our calls. He looked around the lake, then rushed down the hill, got in a fishing boat and sailed towards us. My arms were getting weaker and I could barely keep afloat but we kept calling for help.

The fisherman steered his boat towards us. I held onto it and immediately felt safer, Giguś kept holding on to me, so I focused on looking for Mrs. Z. and Piotruś.

The fisherman checked to make sure we were safe, then sailed towards Mrs. Z. and lifted her with his paddle. She was unconscious, and he dragged her into the boat with great difficulty. Piotruś was not nowhere to be found.

When he heard me shouting that there was a boy as well, he looked around carefully, immersed his paddle a few times, then sailed to us, put us in the boat and, paddling as fast as he could, sailed to the shore, where people were gathering. Mrs. Z. was taken out of the boat and someone immediately tried resuscitate her. A few people jumped in the boat and circled around the site of the accident, looking unsuccessfully for Piotruś. Giguś was sitting on the grass, trembling from the cold and watching the boat with his big, frozen, grey eyes.

"Giguś, run to the house or you'll catch a cold!" I shouted, surprised by my own words. Soon after, I realized that my presence at the shore was unnecessary – they were looking after Mrs. Z, searching for Piotruś and I was just standing there, helpless. I started walking towards the house. Soon I met Mr. Józef, who was running breathless to the place of the accident.

"Miss Zosia, is it true?" he asked, looking into my eyes and gripping my shoulders tightly.

"Yes."

"Go to Ada so she isn't alone and take care of Giga. He is sitting on the stairs looking totally terrified and won't come into the house.

When I got there, Giguś was already dry, wrapped in a blanket and shaking in bed. Mrs. Ada was frozen, numb. She wasn't crying. But the second she saw me, something broke in her. She fell into my arms and embraced me, and we both cried hysterically.

Mrs. Z. was brought to the house, exhausted, pale and in shock. Mrs. Ada wrote a message and asked the co-leaseholder to pass it on to her husband's parents.

Mr. Józef came back after a few hours of ineffective searching for Piotruś.

I didn't know what to do with myself. I thought that I should leave Mrs. Ada and Mr. Józef's presence, but I was aware that difficult times were ahead and that I could be helpful and needed.

Soon, the co-leaseholder came and informed them that the old couple would come in a few hours with Mrs. Ada's sister and brother-in-law. He also passed on a written message from them.

I served everyone hot tea; we were all withdrawn and each processed our enormous pain in our own way.

"Mrs. Ada, if it hurts you to look at me, maybe you'd like me to leave your house?" I tried to explain the situation when we were left alone in the room.

"No, Miss Zosia. Piotruś loves you very much. You understand him so well. You are very close to me. Please don't leave me now." She showed me a message from her in-laws: "Don't punish those who carry God's will. We will be with you soon."

They came in the afternoon. Mr. Józef, Mrs. Ada's father and her brother-in-law got in the boat and sailed off in search of Piotruś. But an hour later they returned and asked me to go with them to show them exactly where the incident had happened. We sailed for quite some time, the lake was calm, and visibility was good, but that didn't help our search.

Suddenly, black clouds rolled in and covered the sky, a strong wind blew and the boat began to wobble on the swelling waves. Nobody said anything. It was terrifying.

"This lake doesn't like Miss Zosia," Grandad said. "We'll let her out at the shore and then we will throw this underwater lighting device in the lake and continue to search. Perhaps his little body is tangled in the seaweed and will surface only when the lake is disturbed."

Meanwhile, a storm was brewing with lightning, thunder and heavy rain. They dropped me off at the shore and told me to go home.

"Don't worry, Miss Zosia, we will call to each other."

I just about managed to get through those bushes to the path and ran home, responding to their calls from time to time.

My appearance at home caused some anxiety as I was soaking wet, full of scratches and my hair was sticking wildly to my face and neck. They thought something bad must have happened at the lake.

We waited until late at night for the men to return. The storm ceased and they didn't come for a long time. Finally, they came back exhausted and shaken – their search had been fruitless.

The next morning was calm, sunny with a cloudless sky. Piotruś's little body was found at the shore; it had probably washed up during the storm.

The funeral and wake came next.

The house was never the same as before.

Mrs. Z. was very ill – she had bilateral aspiration pneumonia. I nursed her. Once she was back on her feet, she left the Święcickis.

I stayed with a heavy heart – I couldn't understand how Mrs. Ada could be warm towards me and often even talk to me about Piotruś.

The co-leaseholder still came in the evenings. Once he brought news about an "action" in the ghetto when lots of people were taken to Ponary and looked troubled while he stared at me.

"They keep taking them but there is no end in sight. They might not be able to kill them all."

"Who knows?" I replied.

I held his look and maintained an indifferent tone which didn't betray what was happening inside of me.

In the autumn, after the Święcickis returned to the city, I had to somehow manage again.

At Auntie's in Antakalnis

At that time, Adzik, who had introduced me to Mrs. Maria Fedecka, Mr. Frąckiewicz and the Wolskis, lived with his wife and friend Tadeusz Chabros in hiding in an old lady's apartment in the suburbs of Vilnius. Because I had no place to stay, he offered me to stay with them for the time being.

The apartment was on the first floor of a wooden house on Antokolska Street, over a working pub, which constantly emitted sounds of drunken singing and rude conversation. The owner of the apartment was an old woman, probably approaching eighty, a pensioner, who lived alone. She was a former shop assistant at the big Saint Wojciech bookstore. I don't know how Adzik knew her nor what deal they had struck with her.

Her name was Mrs. Mackiewiczówna and we called her Auntie. Auntie was small, withered, clean, economical and very physically active for her age. However, we doubted whether she understood the gravity of the situation she had taken on and whether she might in good faith share her experiences, impressions or even fears with "a good neighbor" or "a good friend." To be honest, Auntie didn't keep much of a social life, but she liked to chat with people after a Sunday mass. Which is why, on Saturday evening or Sunday before she left for church, we tried to gently remind her about the necessity of keeping our stay a total secret. Auntie was naïve, a practicing believer but not dogmatic. I think her main motivation for helping us was a desire to earn God's grace.

The main concern was maintaining the appearance that nothing had changed, and that was living alone just like she had for years. But apart from Auntie, there were four more of us at her place. So, naturally, there were certain things we had to do. We needed to make sure no footsteps in the apartment betrayed the presence of more people, we needed to minimize our movement on the staircase, so we walked around the apartment and on the staircase in our socks. Auntie could only buy food for one in the local shops, sometimes she could get away with supplies for two. The rest needed to be somehow smuggled in by other measures.

Adzik's wife had a Semitic look, was pretty and had the understandable characteristics of a person in her situation. She had this look in her eyes, not necessarily one of fear or anxiety, but endless sorrow and surprise that she was innocent but still felt guilty. Różka had also had similar eyes. Such eyes were very "betraying," and anyone with eyes like that could only hide or die. So Lena had a hideout in the loft and if anyone unexpectedly knocked on the door, Lena went inside, one person stayed outside to disguise the hideout and another went slowly down to open the door, stalling if necessary. It happened rarely since none of us, including Auntie, had much of a social life. However, it did happen sometimes. I don't know how Tadek Chabros, a future radio director in Lublin, wound up there. He was Polish, younger than we were, tall and slender with light blond hair. His blue eyes matched his surname[16] very well. He was positive, sometimes even joyful. Tadek dreamed about performing and stubbornly practiced the correct, as he called it, "stage ł"[17] . He was from Warsaw and instead of "ł" he said "eu." He was jealous of our Vilnius "ł," even though we were oblivious to its merits. He took on a vital role in our group – we used him as our 'Aryan banner'. He was introduced as Auntie's nephew who'd come from the countryside. He was sent to the pub under our apartment to get some drinks, and he did so slowly so everyone present could get a good look at him, so this 'Aryan' would be well rooted in the memory of the regulars who were usually drunk, and would be associated with the lodger living over the pub. When the weather was good and sunny, we seated him by an open window facing

16   "chabrowy" in Polish means blue/cornflower blue
17   "ł" – Polish letter/sound

the street, not for the sake of his complexion but as a front. The house was low, the street not very busy, Tadek was good-looking – there was a chance that someone from the opposite houses or one of the few pedestrians would notice him, remember and associate this house with such a man.

Adzik and I tended to provisions and information. Apart from food, we brought news from the city, from the front and from Vilnius. We took trips alone, never in pairs. We went to a district far away, usually to the Wielka Pohulanka area, alongside the Neris River, through the park, in the back of the Vilnius cathedral called Cielętnik and further on through the whole city center. The journey was long and we came back at late dusk with heavily loaded backpacks, just before curfew when there were not many people on the streets and those who yet remained were hurrying to get home. In the evening we shared whatever news we had acquired.

One day Adzik came back with a rumor that people had warned Jews staying on the Aryan side as well as non-Jews with objections to the Germans about a woman who was suspected of spying and reporting to the occupiers.

"Tall, with short hair, usually wearing a skirt and a jacket, flat shoes, she walks with long and vigorous strides, easily and willingly makes contacts with random people on the street," he gave us her description. "Her name is apparently R. Or maybe that's how she introduces herself. Do you understand?" he asked, looking at me.

From that day on, our trips to find food became increasingly more difficult; there was more nervousness and vigilance, more self-doubt, constraint in behavior and the sad awareness that all of this together made everything more dangerous. It felt like a closed circle of feelings and reactions that was weakening our resilience. This was counterbalanced by habit and unavoidable necessity. We simply had no choice – we needed to collect food for three or four people.

More optimistic news was trickling in from the front. The defeat of the fascists was becoming more of a reality. We were all still young and despite tiredness, loss and pain we had suffered, we had a burning urge to survive what was possibly the last stage of the occupation and to once again have a normal life. The hope we felt gave our lives some value after so many years.

Soon after Adzik's warning, when it was my turn to go shopping one day, I stayed in the city a little bit longer and was hurrying home, trying to make the curfew. I was walking with long, fast strides and even though I tried to be quiet, each step seemed to me as loud as a cannon firing. Cielętnik was disappearing in the thick darkness of the old chestnut trees. All at once my steps on the sidewalk didn't seem to be as loud as before – the alleys were not concrete; they were hard soil. I thought that I heard steps behind me.

You're being hysterical! I told myself off in my mind. This didn't stop the steps. I just needed to not turn around and walk calmly – I instructed myself strictly and I must have followed my own command. Only my disobedient heart was beating heavily somewhere in my throat. The steps behind me became clearer, they overlapped with my own and were getting closer. Eventually, on my right-hand side the figure of a woman appeared and caught up with me. Tall, with short hair, in a skirt and jacket and flat shoes. She must have taken very long steps because I'm not short-legged by any means and still she'd caught up. A thought pierced my mind like a shot from a bullet. It's her! I couldn't believe I had run into her! I needed to separate from her before the house at all costs – otherwise everyone would be discovered. But how? What would I do if she didn't go away? The houses on the way were not high and I wouldn't be able to turn into a stairway and wait for her to leave. The owners would notice me and make a scene.

With my head full of thoughts, she turned towards me and looked at me kindly.

"The curfew will start soon," she said calmly, "it's so empty on the street, kind of strange and we are walking in the same direction. It's always better together."

"Yes, of course," I agreed politely.

"Have you got far to go?" she asked.

"Yes, still a little while," I answered, leaving her question unanswered. "And you?"

"I'm turning by the Peter and Paul church."

I'd played it pretty well – I praised myself internally. Now she would have to say goodbye to me by the church while my own "little while" was vague. I'd walk as long as I was sure that no one was following me, I was not even going to think about the curfew.

"Did you hear that something happened in the ghetto again?"

I remembered Adzik's words, 'she makes easy conversation on the street.' Yes, it was her, I was certain. But why such a dramatic topic straight away?

"No, I didn't," I replied, keeping up a guise of indifference.

"Yes, they took people away again, apparently to Ponary."

"How long have we got left until the curfew? I don't have a watch…" I changed the topic.

"Unfortunately, not long, 15-20 minutes. I will make it at the very last minute. And you? If you've got far to go, you can stay overnight at my place."

"Thank you, I'll hurry. My auntie would worry if I didn't return."

"Do you live with an auntie?" she was interested.

"Yes, with an auntie."

We finally passed the church and my companion indeed said goodbye to me. If she lived here, it was not far from us – which couldn't be good news and our separation didn't bring me any relief. Perhaps she would walk through the hedges and spy on me. I looked around carefully, but couldn't see or hear anything. Perhaps it was not her. It was possible – I deliberated within myself, however, I knew I needed to assume the worst.

I passed by our house. There was the compulsory blackout – so I couldn't know what was happening there, were they sleeping soundly? Waiting anxiously for my return? Or something worse?

What could be worse? I tried to be reasonable. She didn't know where I lived. She could only find out now, spying on me.

I crossed the street, then circled back. The street was completely empty. I needed to go home since hanging around near the house might look suspicious.

I opened the front gate to the yard. Quiet. A woodshed, outhouse and some other sheds received me with total indifference. I gave the special knock signal and by the time someone came down, I'd ritually taken off my shoes and was holding them in hand. Helped with my backpack by Adzik, I walked upstairs in my stockings. I felt my appearance gave relief to everyone and to be honest, Tadek's words "we were worried" were unnecessary. As usual, I reported everything and felt the atmosphere in the room thicken.

"At the end of the day, I can't be sure it's her," I concluded.

"I think it's her," said Adzik. "Too many details check out."

We were pensively quiet.

"Well, we need to go to sleep. We won't come up with anything today. We need to sleep on this and then think about what we need to change after what has happened."

Auntie was already sleeping soundly, blissfully unaware of the drama that had unfolded.

The next day we were all thinking the same thing. We couldn't come up with any smart ideas. We simply had no options. After meditations and deliberations, we concluded that for now everything needed to stay the same. Therefore, we were strictly disciplined when it came to keeping the agreed-upon rules at home. Adzik and I took turns going shopping and getting news (getting better – it was already 1944 and Vilnius was liberated from the Nazis in the middle of July 1944). Tadek displayed his Aryan look and practiced his "ł." Auntie bought her allowed food rations nearby and went to church, but only on Sundays and holidays. Lena stayed diligently hidden.

Sometimes Mrs. Wiktoria Grzmielewska came, and because she knew the signal knock, she didn't give us a heart attack. She usually brought something special (mainly hulled grains), news, sometimes just a good mood and an opportunity for an ordinary, normal conversation. This meant a lot in our circumstances.

Time passed. The front was advancing. Auntie brought optimistic news more often from the church about the Nazi army retreating and the Red Army liberating new territories. She mentioned many different informants in her reports. We got confused as to who was who. Auntie's political interests made us nervous but apart from gentle comments and discreet rebukes we couldn't do much about it.

Finally, one Sunday, Auntie came home from church in a euphoric mood. She told us that the front was close and that the Nazis wouldn't stay for long, but reminded us that they still could give us trouble until the very last minute and that's why it was vital to help each other at this time.

"A lady I met in church today told me all this, I think she is a very wise and good woman. I even invited her to pop in one day," she said excitedly. "Her name is Mrs. R."

"Auntie, is this lady young?" asked Tadek, pretending to be just casually curious, but we were all on edge.

"Too old for you," Auntie laughed.

"But is she pretty? What does she look like?" Tadek inquired relentlessly. Auntie described how she looked – it was the spitting image of the woman I'd met!

"Auntie, I'm sure she is a noble person, but we still need to hide Lena so it would be great if you could warn us before she comes," Adzik said.

"And it will be best not to tell her how trusted people knock on our door. We don't tell anyone either," added Tadek, as if we had lots of visitors all the time.

"As you wish. I'll do what you want but really, we should not be afraid of her," she added, sounding slightly offended.

Still, she kept her word. After the next mass we were warned about the visit. On that day, Mrs. R. knocked on the door normally, oblivious to our code. That gave us time to hide Lena, and Tadek and I were appointed to receive the guest. We concluded that it would be better for me to introduce myself as a niece living with an old auntie, in accordance with what I'd said to her that evening.

Obviously, we were both surprised by the meeting as well as relieved. We were recalling that miserable evening. Mrs. R. brought a cake she had baked; Auntie offered tea from her special supplies. Tadek said he'd just come over from the countryside to Auntie for a little bit but would be visiting again and would possibly bring some food from the village. But if he was not able to come again, he might send a cousin – and thus, he opened a door for Adzik's potential appearance in the future.

The visit was moving and warm and ended with Mrs. R. promising that she would visit us again. Things were changing and it was difficult for us to judge the situation, nor could we predict what the future would hold. We blindly muddled along as best we could. After some time, we even "legalized" Adzik. Apart from Lena, she knew all of us. However, we were unsure about what she thought or what her true intentions were.

The front was truly getting closer. An atmosphere of anxiety and uncertainty in the city was growing. We heard that as the Nazis retreated, they burned houses, plundered and made people march in front of them towards the west. People were left considering the best way to survive this chaos of the retreat and the ever-changing frontline.

Mrs. R. visited us again. She was worried and asked what we planned to do. She informed us that some people wanted to leave the city and journey towards the liberating army. Apparently, they would be coming from our side. We would have to go towards Pabrade, Nemencine. She invited us over to her place.

Adzik and I were chosen to go. She lived in a pretty wealthy, wooden house with a neat and organized garden. She offered us tea with jam, which was a Vilnius custom. We chatted; Mr. R. was not there.

"My husband is rarely at home; he gets back from work late. And I actually have something I wanted to talk to you about," she looked at us thoughtfully and continued. "Perhaps you could advise me?" She continued without waiting for our answer. "I have a German deserter hiding in my cellar – he asked for my help and told me he didn't want to fight for Hitler anymore. And as he was telling me, I didn't have the heart to refuse him help. I threw away his clothes and gave him my husband's civilian clothes…" she looked at us inquiringly.

She is provoking us, I thought.

"You know, in such times no one can really give advice. Every individual needs to choose how much they are willing to risk," Adzik said.

"Exactly," she muttered to herself and looked at us piercingly. Or maybe I it was only my imagination. This conversation was not going anywhere.

We felt awkward. However, we tried to be polite and stayed as long as was proper and then we got ready to go home. She walked with us for a bit. I waited again, suspicious. Nothing happened.

"Hard times are coming. We must help each other," Mrs. R. said as we parted.

Auntie had said the same thing.

"Please let me know if you need anything. I'll help if I can," she added unexpectedly.

"Thank you, we will," Adzik replied calmly.

Who was she really? Was she setting us up? Or perhaps she had an inkling of the truth and actually wanted to help? Maybe Auntie, in her naivety, had told her? There was no way to answer those questions.

Meanwhile, the city filled with talk of German soldiers deserting. It became clear that the more losses the Germans suffered, the more cruelly they behaved towards the civilians. Anyone who had family in the countryside tried to leave the city. Some intended to wait until the last minute. But how to time the last minute so that it wouldn't be too late? How to avoid burning houses, being killed at the last minute by a random or unintentional bullet, or being driven to the west? Fear surged in from every direction.

One evening during this nerve-wracking time, just before curfew, we heard knocking on the door. Each person did what they were supposed to without a word, like robots.

"Who is it?" Adzik asked from behind the door.

It was my mom.

"The front is approaching, I was afraid that we would get lost and wanted us to be together so I came," and she cried, probably from nervous exhaustion. Or maybe because she could finally see and touch me. In the morning, Mom said that people were leaving even small towns to go to the forest or villages to wait out the moving front.

We had also considered it but how to do it, how to get Lena out? We decided that we needed to do it a day before or on the very day the battling reached the city. People would be concerned for themselves, and it would be busy and easier to slip by unnoticed.

It had to be the shortest way. The location of our apartment was an advantage in this regard. Common opinion would say that it was best to go towards Nemencine as the Soviet Army was supposedly advancing from that direction. There was still the question of how to get past this short length of road with Lena, from our house to the main road. We seized on a desperate idea. Perhaps we could ask Mrs. R.? Perhaps we'd misjudged her? She'd offered to help. She'd confided in us about a serious matter.

After a few days of consideration, we decided to talk to Mrs. R., and Adzik and I went to see her.

At first, we made small talk about nothing.

"I am happy to see you," she told us with a smile.

"We have missed you too."

"That's nice to hear. Would you like to sit inside or on the balcony? Would you like anything? Tea? Water with squash?"

"Thank you."

Finally, each of us had a glass of water with homemade squash. The pleasantries and politeness were over.

"What are your thoughts on the situation?" she asked us.

"Well, the front will be coming through here in the next few days. What are you planning to do?"

"I don't know. I have not made my mind up, and you?"

"We're leaning rather towards leaving the city. It shouldn't take long - a day or two?"

"Maybe you are right. We should really prepare for this moment now and have a plan to follow quickly later on," she mused.

"Exactly," we agreed.

The conversation fell flat. We didn't know how to get to the point, but eventually I decided to just do it.

"You see, we have some difficulties. We don't want to tempt fate at the last minute."

"What are your concerns? You can speak freely."

"Auntie's nephew from the countryside has left. Auntie doesn't want to move on. Yesterday my mother came as she wants to be with me at this moment. And there is one more person whom we have been helping for some time and can't leave behind."

"Let her go with you."

"The thing is, she is Jewish," Adzik decided to take a leap of faith, "we are afraid to risk her and ourselves and we have no idea how to minimize the potential danger."

Mrs. R got lost in her thoughts.

"Let me think about it, maybe I can help," she said. "Maybe I could take her in for a few days."

"No, we want her to come with us."

"You know, I have a man in mind who could take her out safely, but I'd have to ask him if he would be willing do it. I'll come tomorrow to let you know."

We waited in fear for tomorrow – perhaps they would detain us all? What an idiotic idea it suddenly seemed!

But she arrived the next day in a good mood.

"I have good news for you! He agreed."

"And how will he do it? Who is he?"

"He wears a German uniform because he works for them. He will walk with her wearing this uniform. You three will walk behind them. You will be able to see what's happening the entire way. You can trust me. He won't harm you, don't be afraid. He is my husband. Where is the girl?"

"We don't want to reveal her to anyone yet, not even to you or Auntie. God forbid anything should happen, we would never forgive ourselves."

"How can he take her if he does not know what she looks like?"

"When the day comes to leave the city, he will simply come to us, and we will take him to her."

"All right. Agreed. Let it be done your way."

Once rumors began to spread that the front was approaching Vilnius, we decided to leave the city the next day. We informed Mrs. R.

She came with her husband in the morning. Lena was ready. He took her arm and walked in front. Mom, Adzik and I walked behind them. Very quickly we reached the end of Antokolska Street, and the main road began. Mr. R. and Lena stopped and said goodbye. We arrived next to them and stopped.

"Well, I'm going to say goodbye now. I'm going left to Wołokumpia, and you can go straight through the forest and out of the city."

There was no reason to prolong the conversation, which was why Adzik's next question, given the situation, sounded so strange.

"Were you not scared that you would be stopped? What would you have done?"

"I was ready. I'd equipped myself with a legal order requiring me to report to the office with her," he took a piece of paper out of his pocket. We were not interested in it.

We said goodbye gladly and quickly made our way alongside the main road on the edge of the forest.

The Final Stage

The further we went, the more people appeared – they were leaving the city alone, in groups, in whole families. They were all headed in the same direction – the eastern front.

A few kilometers behind the city we stumbled upon the first peasant houses – more a small settlement than a village. There were lots of people with light luggage around. You could see that they all regarded leaving the city as a brief trip. Some were eating, others were resting on the grass and a few on benches. The residents had no food to share. Everything had been eaten up and drunk by those who had arrived earlier. Only water in a well remained. We decided that Mom and Lena would stay here and Adzik and I would go on to the next villages to get potatoes, even though we had been warned that we might not find anything over there.

It was a beautiful, sunny day, lots of greenery around and it was strange not to feel the fear which had constantly been with us for all those years, even when nothing bad was happening. We walked along a paved road in the middle of a tall, old and sparse forest. Somewhere very high above us pine treetops were swaying gently, creating a continuous game of light and shadows on the grass. It was quiet, all you could hear was natural forest sounds and occasionally a bird tweeted discreetly.

I thought we were still under occupation and at the last minute still anything could happen, but if I was going to paint a picture of "freedom," I think I would paint that forest.

Not far in front of us at a point where the road disappeared around a bend, we suddenly noticed two men, armed and dressed in uniform.

"Who are they? What do we do?" I asked alarmed.

"I don't know. But we have no choice, let's keep walking on this road and meet them," we'd barely exchanged those few words when we heard a loud order.

"Stop! Where are you going?"

"To the village. To get potatoes. We have nothing to eat."

They looked at us suspiciously and commanded again:

"Go quickly, don't look back!"

Off we went. We could recognize from their fading voices that they were headed in the opposite direction.

"What was that?" I asked.

"Don't look back. Probably Vlasov's men. They might shoot you in the back."

We kept walking with bated breath, trying not to change the pace of our march, waiting for that shot to come. The first minute and then the next passed by and nothing happened. We tried to stop ourselves from looking back but eventually our patience ran out, we couldn't wait anymore, we turned around… No one was behind us. We'd made it.

We got potatoes from one of the villages, loaded our backpacks and went back, uncertain whether or not our "friends" had met those fleeing among the houses and whether they had stirred any trouble. But nothing had happened. The crowd around the houses had increased over those last few hours. People sat in groups holding lively discussions. Once we arrived, it turned out they were talking Russian and each group had a Soviet soldier in the center.

We heard some gunfights far off in the city. More soldiers ventured out of the forest. They walked in rows, quite far from each other with guns ready to shoot, looking very serious and focused.

"Stiopa, where?" one of the Soviet soldiers sitting with us called out to one of them.

"To attack," he replied, not even looking to see who had asked the question.

But a soldier running nearby on the road, calling out "help!" and holding his stomach with bloody hands convinced us all that the front had indeed arrived. Soldiers jumped out from a ditch towards him. As they carried him, he lost consciousness and his hands hung heavily by his sides – you could see his bowels through his torn clothes.

Yes, this was the front. We could hear more sounds of battle coming from the city.

Vilnius was liberated on the 16th of July 1944.

I went straight back to the city. It was deserted. It felt like I was the only one there. I vaguely remember my entrance into the city for some unknown reason. Far away, on Pohulanka, near the tollhouse, I was surprised to meet the Święcickis' co-leaseholder. He was the only person I encountered that day. He recognized me from far away. We walked towards each other, and it seemed like he was smiling at me. I recalled his insinuations and the way he had looked for fear or panic in my eyes. When we came together, he greeted me like nothing had happened.

"So, they didn't manage to kill all the Jews," I said, but still I shook hands with him. "I am Jewish. You suspected as much, didn't you?"

"No, why would you say that? I'm sorry, I'm in a rush, I need to say goodbye, someone is waiting for me," he was in such a hurry that this was the last I saw of him.

After that, I didn't meet anyone else. Human corpses lay here and there as well as fallen horses on the deserted roads.

The city and I were free of Nazi occupation.

That day, I destroyed Zosia Januszkiewiczówna's birth certificate and reclaimed my identity with this symbolic act. I became Pola Komaj again. I regret today that I don't have it as a keepsake, but at that moment, the thing I wanted most in the entire world was simply – to be me.

Afterword

All of the names, surnames and places mentioned in this memoir are real. I broke this rule only in two cases: 1.) in the chapter "Summer at Lake Galve" I didn't give Mrs. Z.'s name or surname, because I didn't know them and I can't remember what she was called from the short time we were together; and 2.) Mrs. R. from the chapter "At Auntie's in Antakalnis." This is more complicated: it wasn't clear till the end who she was; how to reconcile Mrs. R.'s husband's German uniform with the crucial help she gave us in the last moments and her support of the German deserter? I think that all assumptions we could make on the subject are pointless and I wouldn't like anyone to do it after reading my book. That's why I refrained from giving Mrs. R.'s true surname.

Thank you so much to all of those who encouraged me to write down my memoir, who assisted me with technical help and shared their photographs.

PHOTOGRAPHS

170

Father, engineer Don Komaj, shortly before the war.

Engineer Don Komaj a few months before his death. The picture was taken for a potential fake identity card.

Mother, Dr. Maria Komaj.

My husband, Dr. Sergiusz Wincygster.

Officially my sister-in-law (my husband's sister) – in reality, a good sister – Rózia Wincygster, lived with us since 1935.

Dr. Pola Wawer – the author.

Wladyslaw Frąckiewicz, technician, my father's co-worker for many years. After the war, a worker at the Institute of Experimental Biology of M. Nenecki in Lodz, and later on in Warsaw, called by others there "a handyman."

172

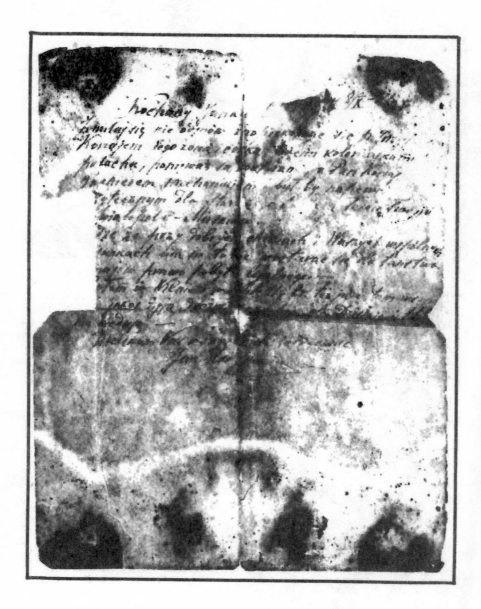

Engineer Jan Hurynowicz's letter to his friend with a plea to help our family.

Sirvintos District Office certificate signed by Mayor Leon Świechowski.

174

Maria Abramowicz-Wolska, linguist, Feliks Wolski, lawyer and art historian.
After the war – employees of the Polish Embassy in Italy; after that Mrs. Maria –
Russian language lecturer at the Warsaw University, Mr. Feliks – employee of the
Ministry of Culture.
Awarded the Righteous Among the Nations Medal (without my influence).

Wiktoria Grzmielewska who taught Szmer-
ka Kaczergiński how to be "mute."
Szmerka Kaczergiński – Jewish language
poet; he died after the war in a plane crash.

My medical certificate after my wartime adventures.

Doctor Janina Jantzen, who gave me an authentic Russian birth certificate for my mother. After the war she worked as a children's rheumatologist at the Paediatric Clinic in Szczecin.

Professor and doctor Ksienia Lutomska. She organized and ran the Dental Clinic MA[18] in Gdansk. Our friendship lasted from the fourth year of our studies until the end of her life.

Doctor Emilia Pogorzelska – assistant and later associate professor of the Pediatric Clinic MA in Łódź.

Docent / Dr. Wojciech Pogorzelski – director of the Psychiatric Clinic MA in Łódź.

18   MA – Medical Academy

My mom, Zosia and Emilia Pogorzelska.

My mom as a nanny.

*Zosia Pogorzelska –
soon after the war.*

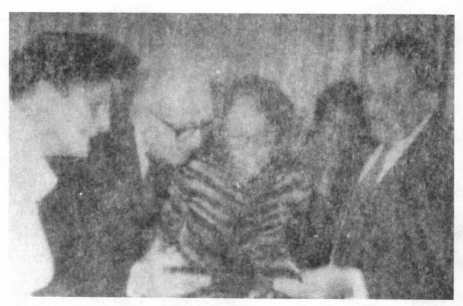

Awarding the Righteous Among the Nations Medal by the first Israeli Ambassador to Poland, Mordechai Palzur.

A meeting with professor and doctor Chaim Hilel Fryd almost half a century after the war and over half a century of friendship. Tel-Aviv, 1988.

Olga Łokuciewska – our friendship lasted until her last days.
She died on the 9th of October 1989.

Bronislaw Łokuciewski –the "director"
of my stay in Koziełłowszczyzna.

Docent Maria Rzeuska, Polish teacher – she is seated at the bottom, in the middle, wearing a striped blouse at the USB (the Stefan Batory University) philosophy seminar. Thanks to her I met Marysia Markowska and later on the Święcickis – this helped with over half a year of my war life.

Ada Święcicka – painter; after the war she worked for many years with "Przyjaciolka".

Józef Święcicki – journalist. Arrested in July 1945 by Soviet authorities, died in 1946 in a camp in Inta, the Vorkuta region.

Ada and Józef Święcicki's boys:
Mateusz is sitting behind the armchair,
a future contemporary music composer
and musician. Died in 1985.
Piotruś is sitting in the armchair, and
"Giga" is sitting on the armrest – Jan
Święcicki, pediatrician.

Piotruś Święcicki, born 28.06.1936,
drowned 23.07.1943.

CPSIA information can be obtained
at www.ICGtesting.com
Printed in the USA
LVHW100621191122
733282LV00006B/134

9 789655 752861